The Political Life and Times of
MATILDA JOSLYN GAGE

For Heather
With Peace, Love, +
Sisterhood!

Mary E Corey

The Political Life and Times of
MATILDA JOSLYN GAGE

Activist, Historian, Publisher, Writer

MARY E. COREY

Paramount Market Publishing, Inc.

Paramount Market Publishing, Inc.
274 North Goodman Street, Suite D-214
Rochester, NY 14607
www.paramountbooks.com
607-275-8100

Publisher: James Madden
Editorial Director: Doris Walsh

Cover image: *Woman at writing desk,* oil on canvas, Lesser Ury, 1898, courtesy of WikiArt.

Cataloging in Publication Data available
ISBN-10: 1-941688-60-8 | ISBN-13: 978-1-941688-60-1 *paper*
eISBN: 978-1-941688-61-8

Contents

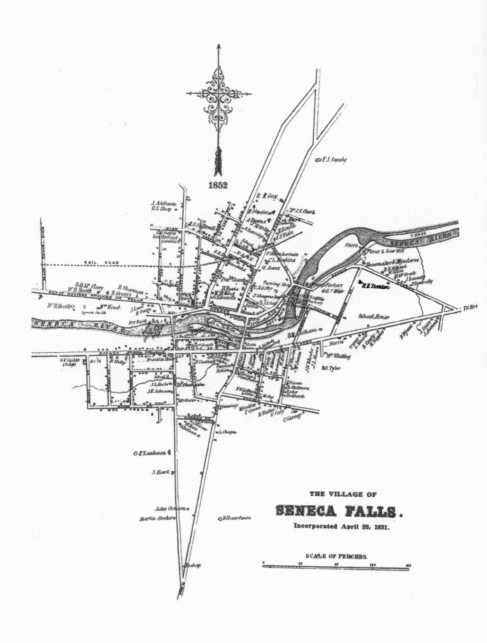

1852

THE VILLAGE OF

SENECA FALLS.

Incorporated April 22, 1831.

SCALE OF PERCHES.

Introduction

Picture it, Sunday night, March 29, 1953, 6:30. Families all across the country have finished their dinners and settled in to watch *You Are There* with Walter Cronkite. That night he would be taking us into the distant past to, with his stentorian basso, invite us to watch unfold "a day like all days, filled with those events that alter and illuminate our times, and *you are there*." On this night "The Witch Trial of Salem" alternately fascinated and repulsed us. How could people think like that? Act like that? For me, a wide-eyed eight-year-old, it resonated. I didn't understand exactly what there was about it that struck a nerve but it stayed with me. Much later Miss Smith, my high school history teacher, convinced me that the past was the key to the future. Unlocking the past, she always said, was the key to all our futures.

Walter Cronkite,
You Are There,
CBS

Fast forward to graduate school and the daunting task of finding just the right topic for my dissertation research. As a firm believer in the "stroll around the library and read the titles" school of research, I hit on the woman suffrage movement as a possibility. I knew I wanted it to be in the field of women's history and since I was from Seneca Falls,

it seemed a natural fit. As I strolled through the stacks, I remember lingering as I read the names on the spine of *The History of Woman Suffrage* and noticing that even though I knew Stanton and Anthony, I wasn't as sure about who Gage was. A stop at a local bookstore helped answer my question. There it was! a reprint of *Woman, Church and State*, by Matilda Joslyn Gage, a book I'd met years earlier. This time the cover illustration was a bright red flame. Hard to miss. Was this the same Gage as the Gage on the spine of the *History?* Of course, it was.

I first met Gage in the college library in a book that hadn't been checked out in years. I was looking for answers to a question that would be central to a paper I was working on for an undergraduate class on the history of the middle ages. Perhaps that long-ago television show had something to do with my topic. My question was: What caused the "burning time," the centuries of witchcraft trials and thousands upon thousands of women burned at the stake? Only Gage offered a credible answer. She argued way back in 1893 that all other interpretive considerations paled in light of the overwhelmingly gender-specific nature of the persecutions: ". . . as soon as a system of religion was adopted which taught the greater sinfulness of woman, [the doctrine of the fall] the persecution for witchcraft became chiefly directed against women . . . When for "witches" we read "women," we gain fuller comprehension of the cruelties inflicted . . ." That's it! That's the answer!

You could think of it as expanding all the alternative theses and adding "so they burned midwives/mothers/beautiful women/old women, etc." It would sound like this: The economy was in peril, so they burned midwives/mothers/beautiful women/old women, etc. Or disease was rampant, so they burned midwives/mothers/beautiful women/old women. You see how disingenuous (silly) that sounds. Modern scholars have, to be sure, modified and clarified her assertions but none have overturned them.

Running into her again so soon after my stroll in the library, now in the Persephone Press edition, was my own personal "aha!" moment. Way before there was such a thing as women's history, Gage was writing it and I wanted to know more. This was going to be the start of a beautiful friendship.

Our story about Matilda Joslyn Gage, however, starts in 1852, not a particularly important year, except for a few notable moments and one infamous event. Early in the year Mt. Sinai Hospital was founded in New York City by a group of Jewish charitable organizations and the Studebaker Wagon Company began rolling out the wagons that would carry thousands of homesteaders west. *Uncle Tom's Cabin* was published in 1852.

A shameful event occurred in mid-April: the massacre of over 150 native people by an over-zealous sheriff, William H. Dixon and seventy of his boys, in Trinity County, California. It became known as the Bridge Gulch Massacre or the Natural Bridge Massacre.

On July 1, Henry Clay, the author of the American Plan, died and became the first to be accorded the honor of lying in state in the United States Capitol Rotunda. On the Fourth of July, Frederick Douglass delivered his bombshell of a speech, "The Hypocrisy of American Slavery" to a stunned audience in Rochester, New York. August 3 saw the first boat race between Harvard and Yale, the first intercollegiate athletic competition.

In November, Democrat Franklin Pierce defeated Whig Winfield Scott for the presidency and would go on to not distinguish himself in the office.

Also, in 1852, planters in Hawaii began bringing in Chinese contract laborers to work 12-hour days, 6 days a week, on their sugar plantations for a whopping $3 a month plus room and board. Loyola College was chartered in Maryland and Tufts University was founded in Massachusetts.

But, an event that won't be found on any of the timelines for the year 1852 was the entrance into the woman suffrage ranks of Matilda Joslyn Gage at the Syracuse Convention. In fact, the convention itself goes unremarked. However, the September, 1852, Syracuse, New York, Women's Rights Convention brought the first appearance of the woman who would go on to become one of the most forward thinking, dynamic leaders the suffrage movement would ever know. Unfortunately, the biases and inaccuracies that dominated how her work was appraised and valued at the turn of the 20th century, cloaked her grand vision and did a huge disservice to us all. How did this happen? You'll have to read on to find out.

She wasn't scheduled to speak that day and was unknown to the gathered crowd but she bravely approached the podium "when her courage had reached a sufficiently high point, [and] with palpitating heart she ascended the platform, where she was cordially given place by Mrs. Mott . . . [1] Mrs. Mott later recalled that Gage was "trembling in every limb" as she spoke. But, in spite of her obvious nervousness she had much to say.

"This convention has assembled to discuss the subject of woman's rights, and form some settled plan of action for the future. Then with a rhetorical flourish proclaimed, "Let Syracuse sustain her name for radicalism!"[2] Radicalism? With these words Gage launched her forty-six-year career in women's rights as a speaker, activist, and historian. In this first speech to a suffrage convention she articulated all of the themes her later work would embody and revealed the historian's perspective that she would bring to all her speeches and writings.

The Speech

In her judgment, women's situation was an historic construct desperately in need of radical reconstruction. Woman's position, she said, was like the "mass of mankind" when "science and learning were in the hands of the priests, and property held by vassalage; . . . education was held to be unfit for the masses, while the tenure of their landed property was such as kept them in a continual state of dependency on their feudal lord." Woman's sphere, she argued, was not and should not be considered any more static or immutable than the situation of other formerly dependent groups. Implicitly she offered woman's situation agency and historical process; agency in the option to strive for change and process in the precedents of the past.

Her historian's eye also offered a usable past to give witness to the many accomplishments of women, in spite of their imposed disabilities caused by a lack of educational opportunities, and oppressive religious dogma permeating their traditional role and insinuating itself into their legal status. Without denying the progress yet to come, Gage insisted that women needed a knowledge of their collective past – achievements not just oppression.

To refute the prevailing wisdom that women were unfit for worldly spheres, she spoke of governing women "from Semiramis to Victoria;" the scientific genius of women like Helena Lucretio Corano, Mary Cunitz, and Caroline Herschell; literary giants such as Sappho, Joannie Baille, Margaret Fuller, and Harriet Beecher Stowe. Great women, she argued, could be found in every avenue of learning: "languages, history, poetry, music, painting, mathematics, astronomy, drama, and politics."

As she continued speaking she took a hard look at the laws surrounding the legal fiction that "after marriage, the husband and wife are considered as one person in law . . ." This, she declared, was false "from the very laws applicable to married parties. Were it so, the act of one would be as binding as the acts of the other, and wise legislators would not need to meet to enact statutes defining the peculiar rights of each; were it so a woman could not legally be a man's inferior." With excitement mounting, she continued, "In laws determining inheritance rights, the custody of children, real and personal property, as well as wages, married women are classed with 'idiots, persons of unsound mind, and infants!' *Well classed, truly!*"

Children, that quintessential part of woman's proper sphere, even children were also legally beyond any real control by their mothers. "Every father has a right to bind, or give away, any of his children, while minors, without the consent, or even the knowledge of their mother. When he dies, she's not considered a competent guardian . . . in his will or deed, [he can] exclude the mother from participation in such guardianship." He could exert his control even from the grave.

To those who claimed women desired no such rights or claimed they had enough of them already, she challenged, ". . . converse with any intelligent women on the subject, and you will not find them indifferent . . . An ignorant woman is virtually in the same condition as the peasant who thinks it right that a king shall rule over him; and to keep him content, he is made to believe it would be a blasphemy and treason in him to call into question this right." Religious arguments against woman's rights were answered with reference to the Bible reminding the orthodox, "He created man in his own image, after his own likeness, both; male and female, and gave them equal dominion."

Her impatience with entrenched orthodoxy was obvious when she asked, ". . . how can this mental and moral lethargy, which so binds the generality of women, be shaken off?" Her answer, "Self-reliance is one of the first lessons to be taught our daughters; they should be educated with our sons and equally with them taught to look forward to some independent means of support."

Implicitly she gave witness to the idea that women can and must use, manipulate, and interpret the wisdom of the past in their own best self-interest. She was not impressed by a republic "making great professions in regard to general liberty, yet the right to particular liberty, natural equality, and personal independence, of two great portions is treated, from custom with the greatest contempt; color in the one instance and sex in the other are brought as reasons why they should be derided . . ."³ Lucretia Mott was so impressed by this speech from a nervous newcomer that she arranged for Gage's speech to be published with the other convention addresses.

Central New York Beginnings

Although new to the organized women's rights movement, Gage was familiar with the general reform movements that grew out of the Second Great Awakening. Born in 1826 in Cicero, New York, heart of the "burned over district," her parents, Dr. Hezekiah and Helen Leslie Joslyn, were "sympathetic to the reforms of the time, abolition, temperance, woman's rights, and free thought. Their home was a gathering place for reformers and a stop on the Underground Railroad."[4] Dr. Joslyn was also one of the founders of the anti-slavery Liberty Party, as was Elizabeth Cady Stanton's husband, Henry. As a child and young woman, she was educated at home by her father in such subjects as "physiology, Greek, and mathematics and taught to think for herself." At sixteen she attended the Clinton Liberal Institute in Clinton, New York, to complete her education in anticipation of attending medical school. Her father petitioned for her entrance to Geneva Medical School, his *alma mater*, in 1843 and 1844 but she was rejected both times because she was a woman.

Instead, at the age of eighteen, Matilda Joslyn chose a more conventional path, and married Henry Hill Gage, a Cicero merchant, on January 6, 1845. Henry Gage was sympathetic to reform, but more interested in running a busy dry goods store. He supported his wife's work, however. As stated in his obituary, "Although taking much interest in political questions, Mr. Gage gave his first attention to business." As a young married couple, they moved several times, first from Cicero to Syracuse, then to Manlius, finally settling in nearby Fayetteville, New York where Henry Gage opened H.H. Gage Dry Goods Store. They had five children; four of which survived to adulthood.

From 1852 on, Matilda Joslyn Gage participated in petition drives for women's rights in Syracuse and the Onondaga County area. Local newspapers chronicled her speaking engagements at women's rights and abolition conventions in Syracuse, Rochester, Saratoga, and smaller towns in upstate New York. During the years before and during the Civil War she became closely allied with Elizabeth Cady Stanton and Susan B. Anthony, and increasingly well known in reform circles.[5] After the Civil War she joined the American Equal Rights Association. When the rift between those who were unwilling to risk defeat of "Negro" suffrage, Lucy Stone and Henry Blackwell and those who could not support a Fifteenth Amendment that did not include woman suffrage, Stanton, Anthony, and Gage, ended that organization she joined Anthony and Stanton to organize the National Woman Suffrage Association in May, 1869. She agreed with Anthony on the need for state suffrage associations to support the National and drew up an ambitious plan of organization for New York State that became the model for organizing successive state organizations.[6]

From NWSAs beginnings, Gage was continuously elected to top-tier NWSA offices. She and Anthony rotated in the positions of Chair of the Executive Committee, Chair of the Committee on Resolutions, and the Vice-presidency, while Stanton dominated the Presidency. Gage was elected president of NWSA for one term, 1875–76, and served as president of the New York State Woman Suffrage Association for five years, 1870-75. Thereafter she served continuously as either vice-president or Chair of the Executive Committee of NYSWSA until her death in 1898.

Becoming Visible, Getting Dramatic

During her years with NWSA her stature grew with her every involvement in some of NWSA's most visible and dramatic public moments. Here's an example of her response to the less enlightened: In 1872, a small anti-suffrage organization led by Mrs. Adm. Dahlgren and Mrs. Gen. William T. Sherman published their views opposing women's enfranchisement because, "Holy scripture inculcates a different, and for us higher, sphere apart from public life." They then presented a proposal for a Sixteenth Amendment to Congress that would empower Congress to "legislate uniform national laws regulating and restricting marriage, divorce, dower rights, and marriage and birth registrations." Gage, as Chair of the Committee on Arrangements, promptly invited Dahlgren and Sherman to NWSA's Washington convention. "Nothing," she wrote, "would afford the officers . . . greater pleasure than to hold a debate . . . with yourselves and your friends." She even promised Elizabeth Cady Stanton would "enter the list against them." The ladies, of course, declined claiming, "[debate] on a public platform . . . ignores the principle that ourselves and our friends seek to defend, viz., the preservation of female modesty." Apparently, they didn't consider publishing their views and presenting their petition to Congress violations of their "female modesty."[7]

While Stanton disapproved of Anthony's decision to vote in the 1872 presidential election, Gage supported her. After Anthony's arrest and the change in venue for her trial from Monroe County to Ontario County, it was clear that a canvass of Ontario County was necessary.

Anthony and woman suffrage issues weren't as well known outside of Monroe County. Gage came to Anthony's aide, wrote her speech, "Is it a Crime for a U.S. Citizen to Vote" and together they divided the county and went on a whirlwind speaking tour to get their views before both the public and the potential jury pool. Gage stayed by Anthony's side throughout the trial, lending her moral support and documenting the proceedings.

As Chair of the Committee on Resolutions, she was the author and driving force behind the most notable and controversial of the NWSA's resolutions, The Rochester Resolutions. NWSA had a well-earned reputation for flamboyant conventions and hard-driving resolutions. The Rochester Resolutions offered at the Thirtieth Anniversary Convention held in Rochester in 1878 set off a storm of protest from the general circulation newspapers and pulpits nationwide, in particular the three resolutions aimed at the "Christian Church's crimes against women."[8]

1876 was the nation's centennial but where was democracy or republican government for women one hundred years after the revolution? NWSA was determined to ask that question publicly at the official celebrations in Philadelphia. Rebuffed in their attempts to secure a place in the program, they decided to present their Declaration of Rights unofficially. With a few tickets into the main ceremonies Anthony, Gage, Lillie Devereux Blake, Sara Andrews Spencer, and Phoebe Couzins waited eagerly in their seats waiting for an opportune moment. Seizing a pause in the program, they quickly hustled to the stage and right up to the podium and a very startled Vice-president Thomas W. Ferry and presented their declaration. Later, flushed with their daring, Gage held a parasol to shade Anthony from the July sun while she read their declaration to a "listening and applauding crowd" in front of Independence Hall.[9]

Ten years later, Gage, Blake, and the other officers of the NYSWSA protested the dedication of the Statue of Liberty. Gage proclaimed it "the sarcasm of the nineteenth century to represent liberty as a woman, while not one single woman throughout the length and breadth of the land is as yet in possession of political liberty!"[10] They were not to be deterred by a mere warning from the organizers of the ceremonies. They made it clear: "There will be NO women in the gathering on the island, at least it is hoped not. No tickets have been issued to ladies, and if any of the fair sex are present on the island at the unveiling it will be the result of their persistency . . . .[11] They were persistent! Within a few short weeks they rented a steamship, raised their protest banners, (literally) barged into the official flotilla, and delivered their speeches.

Our Historian

As delightful as the stories of her participation in some of the more out-rageous moments in the usually quite decorous history of the NWSA are, Gage's weightier contribution to the movement rests on her scholarship. She can best be assessed as an historian, a pioneering advocate of women's history, and the author of the only monograph on women's history to emerge from the 19th-century suffrage movement. In many ways, our first women's historian. From her first speech at the Syracuse Convention in 1852 to the publication of her magnum opus, *Woman, Church and State,* her speeches, writings, and advocacy were and remain an education in women's history. Her work was based on careful research, well documented, and written with a characteristically scholarly tone. William Leach declared, "Matilda Joslyn Gage, perhaps the most important of all nineteenth-century femi-nist historians, ceaselessly mined the past for material on gifted women."[12] Leach is right, but to be clear, there were no other women's historians at that time in the sense that we use that word today, Gage would not have recognized the term "feminist" and her research is so valuable to us today because, although she did study gifted women, she was equally or more interested in the situation of ordinary women.

Today the work of this gifted woman as an advocate, activist, intel-lectual, and leader is finally being acknowledged in larger ways. She is no longer such a ghostly figure in the secondary literature of the suffrage movement, no longer a somewhat vaguely familiar name. This is encouraging. But, she still deserves to be not just somewhat famil-iar but fully restored to the prominent position she held in life. And, because her story is so closely woven into the history of the NWSA, Stanton, and Anthony, restoring Gage also bears weighty insights into their stories too.

The heart of this research digs into Gage's contributions to the NWSA as its chronicler, as a prominent officer for over forty years, and as its historian. Chapter one, *Matilda Gage, Take the Stage* describes the process that wrote Gage into the margins of the movement at the end of the 19th century and early 20th century. For this we take a close look at the published works produced under the direction of Susan B. Anthony and written by her amanuensis, Ida Husted Harper. The Anthony volumes were mirrored by the self-congratulatory works by Elizabeth Cady Stanton and further revised by her children. In the Stanton volumes, the star of the show is always Stanton; even Anthony moves to the sidelines. Without challenging these accounts they were then (too) closely followed by historians in the latter part of the 20th century as they began reconstructing the work of their suffrage grand-mothers. Ironically, in the day-to-day documents of both Anthony and Stanton, Gage figures most prominently. So, dig we must if we're going to get a better view of Gage's work and her relationship to the other leaders of the movement.

Chapter two, *Revolution to National Citizen, Gage Ink,* focuses on the first of these contributions – her years in the woman suffrage press. Beginning with her writings for Anthony's paper, *Revolution,* along with her contributions to the full range of suffrage newspapers, and ultimately her work as writer and editor of the official newspaper of the NWSA, *The National Citizen and Ballot Box.* Prominent historian, Ellen DuBois, called it "a major suffrage newspaper," but it has received very little attention.[13] In the years since DuBois's comment was published in 1980, Gage's work has become more widely known. But, analysis of *The National Citizen and Ballot Box,* has still been limited. Actually, most of the suffrage press waits for further exploration. Chapter two will help fill that gap.

Chapter three, *Writing the History of Woman Suffrage,* takes the reader on a ten-year journey through the day-to-day activities of Stanton, Gage, and Anthony as they labored on behalf of woman suffrage and compiled and wrote the *History of Woman Suffrage,* volumes I-III. This was the most rewarding research because it brought to light just how these three volumes, so lovingly created, came to be. I've already mentioned some of the ways that Gage has not received her due. This chapter lays to rest any lingering doubts about her contributions as a writer to these volumes, her diligence, her prominence, or her value to the movement. Searching for a true estimation of Gage's work, happily offered not only insights into her own schedule, family life, and work, but a fascinating view of the work, families, and schedules of all three. This is, in and of itself, worth the price of admission.

Chapter four, *What Could Possibly Go Wrong?* goes behind the scenes for the intrigue that effected the merger of the NWSA with the American Woman Suffrage Association. 1890 was a bitter year for many NWSA members as their beloved association was quite suddenly merged with their old rivals, AWSA to become the hybrid National American Woman Suffrage Association. As awkward as that name sounds, equally awkward was the resultant organization. Neither as radical as the NWSA in its heyday, nor as staid as the AWSA, the new vanilla association limped along into a decade labeled "the doldrums" by future historians. Gage led the opposition to the merger but when it became clear the merger could not be stopped, she, and others, stung by the machinations to effect the merger, left. The methods used were to her mind the exact antithesis of the ideals of the old NWSA and she felt she could never participate comfortably in the new association, nor did it seem to her that her life-long co-adjutors wanted her to.

Leaving NWSA was a hard pill for Gage to swallow, but it did not end her career. Chapter five explores her work as an historian and the writer of the only monograph on women's history to come out of the 19th-century woman's movement. After trying her hand at organizing a new liberal association, she refocused her attention on her life's research into woman's situation over time at the hands of both church doctrine and states craft. The result was *Woman, Church, and State, The Original Expose of Male Collaboration Against the Female Sex.* It also chronicles the mending of fences with Stanton and her work on *The Woman's Bible.* Unlike many in the suffrage movement, Gage's vision was much broader than mere suffrage, she wanted to upend patriarchy. In this she was very much aligned with Stanton's philosophy and a stalwart contributor to Stanton's revising committee. As she explained, "As the first process towards becoming well is to know that you are ill, one of the principle aims of the *National Citizen* is to make those women discontented who are now content . . ." Gage and Stanton were very good at making the contented discontented.

Chapter six, *The end? Not yet!* Gage had a rich family life beyond her political career and Chapter Six takes a brief excursion into this more personal side of Gage's life. Although the focus of this research is her role in the suffrage movement, she pursued her career while raising four children, a situation that working women can readily relate to. Much of what we know about her career can only be found in her letters to her children, especially her eldest son and daughter, T.C. (Thomas Clarkson) and Helen Leslie so her suffrage activities are woven into letters also filled with family life. This side of Gage adds a necessary scope of depth, warmth, and humor to the historian and activist of the preceding chapters.

One purpose for recovering the work of Matilda Joslyn Gage as a writer and historian, as well as an activist, is to bring to the fore one of the most dynamic women of her, or any, century. We could use her quick wit and sharp analysis today. Recovering Gage's place also offers a somewhat less reverential analysis of Susan B. Anthony and Elizabeth Cady Stanton, a necessary corrective to the singular place in the woman suffrage movement that they now command. The quicksand of "great woman" history is as fraught with danger as that of the "great man" school. By following Gage's work, we will be able to add weighty substance to the faint praise she's received by historians and rather see clearly the priceless value of her work editing the *National Citizen,* writing the *History of Woman Suffrage*, and her work as an activist and historian. That Stanton, and in particular Anthony, lose a bit of luster is all to the good. They don't need our accolades or fawning admiration – they need us to see them for the dynamic, albeit human, figures that they were.

NOTES

1. Elizabeth Cady Stanton, Susan B. Anthony, Matilda Joslyn Gage, *History of Woman Suffrage*, (New York: Fowler & Wells, 1881-1886 I-III).

2. Matilda Joslyn Gage, "Speech of Mrs. M. E. J. Gage at the Woman's Rights Convention, Held at Syracuse, Sept., 1852" (Glen Rock, N.J.: Microfilming Corp. of America, 1975).

3. *Ibid.*, All above-quoted material is from this first speech.

4. Dwight H. Bruce, ed., *Onondaga's Centennial*, vol. I, (Boston: Boston History Co., 1896).

5. Anthony to Gage, Dec. 5, 1854, April 21, 1856, Feb. 1862, Gage Collection, Schlesinger Library. Membership in the Onondaga Equal Rights Assoc., American Anti-Slavery Society then American Equal Rights Assoc., Woman's Rights Convention. She was a regular speaker at the conventions of all of the organizations in which she was involved. She joined and stayed in the upper echelons; always "on the platform."

6. Gage, "Appeal to the Friends of Woman Suffrage in the State of New York," *Revolution*, July 29, 1869, 49.

7. *History of Woman Suffrage*, II, 494-5.

8. *HWS*, III, 124-5 These three resolutions will be discussed later.

9. *HWS*, III, 27-15

10. Katherine Devereus Blake and Margaret Louise Wallace, *Champion of Women, The Life of Lillie Devereux Blake* (New York: Fleming H. Revell Co., 1943) 165.

11. *New York Herald*, Oct. 28, 1886, 1; and Sally Roesch Wagner, A Time of Protest, (Sacramento, Calif.: Spectrum Publications, 1987) 112.

12. William Leach, *True Love and Perfect Union*, (New York: Basic Books, 1980) 162.

13. Ellen DuBois, *Feminism and Suffrage: The Emergence of an Independent Women's Movement in America 1848-1869*, (Ithaca: Cornell University Press, 1980) 182, n. 56.

CHAPTER 1

Matilda Gage, Take the Stage

THE struggle to obtain the vote for women remains the longest-lived, singular cooperative political effort in the history of American women. It's safe to say that the beginnings of women's drive for equality stretches back into farthest mists of time. Yes, we know that throughout the ages exceptional women, brave women, women of great intellect, women of great talent have always struggled to have a place at the table on an equal footing with men of the same or even lesser talents. But today, we date the beginnings of the organized struggle for woman suffrage to the meeting between Elizabeth Cady Stanton and Lucretia Mott at the London Abolitionist's convention. Barred from speaking and forced to watch the "menfolk" do all the talking from behind a curtain,[1] they instead talked to each other. From that experience the two friends would lay the earliest groundwork

for woman suffrage in the United States. As luck would have it for me, they arranged to hold their first convention in Seneca Falls, New York, my hometown and the place where Stanton was then living.

How odd to realize I grew up in the heart of the woman suffrage movement but that it was truly hidden in plain sight. I attended Elizabeth Cady Stanton Elementary School, there was an historical marker in honor of the first woman suffrage convention in front of the laundromat downtown

Above: Elizabeth Cady Stanton
Elementary School, Garden Street,
Seneca Falls

Center: New York State Historical
Marker, corner of Fall and Mynderse
Streets, Seneca Falls

Below: Elizabeth Cady Stanton's house,
32 Washington Street, Seneca Falls,
as it appeared in the 1950s.

and another one commemorating Elizabeth Cady Stanton in front of my friend Margaret's house on Washington Street. But that was the sum extent of the remnants of that earth-shattering day in July 1848 when those gathered proclaimed "That all men and women were created equal." You would have thought the glow would have lasted forever. It didn't. The lingering embers of that momentous occasion would have to wait until the 1970s to be coaxed back into life again. Ours were not the only embers that began glowing again. All over the country women who had marched against the Vietnam War, marched for civil rights, were now marching for women's rights. The few bits and pieces of our history became the digs for our past. Like anthropologists we began sifting through the rubble of our lost movement looking for the relics that we could use to build on. We found the *History of Woman Suffrage*, Stanton's *Eighty Years and More, The Life of Susan B. Anthony*, and a few other tomes that had been written to chronicle the early woman suffrage years. We also relied on copies of Anthony's *Revolution*, the *Declaration of Sentiments*, and a wealth of other suffrage newspapers, among them the *National Citizen and Ballot Box*.

From the first convention in Seneca Falls on July 19, 1848 to the final signature on the Nineteenth Amendment, August 26, 1920, this struggle had defined women's rights activism for seventy-two years. Not one of the pioneering leaders of the movement lived to cast a ballot, and that is one of the most admirable measures of their persistence. With little progress to sustain them, these women of the 19th century, Elizabeth Cady Stanton, Lucretia Mott, Susan B. Anthony, Lucy Stone, Matilda Joslyn Gage, Isabella Beecher Hooker, Lillie Devereux Blake, and too many others to count, pledged their lives, their fortunes, and their sacred honor to achieving this monumental and necessary foundation for full citizenship and equality for American women.

Determined that the story of their efforts would not be lost, they assiduously recorded everything. During the two decades immediately following the passage of the woman suffrage amendment a number of celebratory biographies by "friends of" and "daughters of" the principals also hurried to preserve the recent past, and in the case of Elizabeth Cady Stanton, rescue her work from becoming a mere footnote to the record of Susan B. Anthony. Anna Hollowell edited *The Life and Letters of James and Lucretia Mott*. Alice Stone Blackwell preserved her mother's memory in *Lucy Stone: Pioneer for Women's Rights*. Lillie Devereux Blake's daughter, Katherine, and Louise Wallace published *Champion of Woman: The Life of Lillie Devereux Blake*. Abigail Scott Duniway wrote *Path Breaking* and Florence Howe Hall commemorated her mother in *Julia Ward Howe*. Most have since been forgotten.

For a movement so focused on remembering, it's telling how so much was purposefully forgotten. One of these forgettings, a story that seems hard to believe today, is the near erasure of Elizabeth Cady Stanton. When the 19th Amendment was finally ratified in 1920, it was immediately christened the *Susan B. Anthony Amendment* in spite of the fact that the first rendition of it was written by Stanton and Mott. In part an explanation can be found in the wranglings and enmity over the merger of NWSA and AWSA in 1889 and the huffy reaction by the NAWSA women to Stanton's *Bible* a few years later. And, in part it can be ascribed to the ascendance of Anthony at the end of the century. Through the political strategy of gathering to herself a coterie of devoted acolytes, Anthony ultimately controlled the agenda and memory of the early suffrage movement. As first one then another of the early pioneers passed, Anthony became the public face of woman suffrage.

Kneeling, Miss Alice Paul, vice president of National Woman's Party, and Miss Anita Pollitzer, national secretary, laying a tribute of flowers on the grave of Susan B. Anthony, Mount Hope cemetery, Rochester.

Where's Elizabeth Cady Stanton?

A measure of how completely Stanton was lost can be found in the proceedings of the 75th anniversary of the first suffrage convention. The festivities were held in Seneca Falls in 1923 but none of the pageantry celebrated Stanton's role in that first convention. Instead the conventioneers made a pilgrimage to Anthony's grave in Rochester and completely ignored the opportunity to take what would have been a short walk to Washington Street and Stanton's former home. How could the National Woman's Party organizers have overlooked the reason why that first convention was held in Seneca Falls? It presents the strange contradiction of being held in Seneca Falls because of its historical importance while at the same time ignoring that it had that importance because Elizabeth Cady Stanton lived there.[2] It reflected the uneasy past. At that time jockeying between the post-suffrage organizations and personalities (in particular Alice Paul and Stanton's daughter Harriet Stanton Blatch) left Stanton and her role in the suffrage movement contested territory for them and a foggy memory for most others. Stanton's rightful legacy was at the time controlled by her daughter, Blatch and she was not about to let Paul and the NWP use that legacy for themselves. So, in spite of the clear connection between Stanton and Seneca Falls, Paul and the National Woman's Party instead claimed SBA as their historical antecedent.

Organizers of the event planned to use Seneca Falls to establish their legitimacy as rightful suffrage heirs by forging a direct line between the first women's suffrage convention and their own to bring a sense of symmetry to their own convention. The main highlight of the event was to be the introduction by The National Women's Party of their proposed Equal Rights Amendment. In the weeks ahead of the convention a crescendo of enthusiastic advertising about the convention poured from the pages of *Equal Rights*, the newspaper of the National Women's Party. The irony of using the historical significance of Seneca Falls and at the same time minimizing the importance of Elizabeth Cady Stanton is an apt example of the role of contested memory in the interpretive records of the movement and its leaders. In the years between the adoption of the *Susan B. Anthony Amendment* and the introduction of the Equal Rights

Amendment, Stanton, was still acknowledged as the "intellectual leader of the early suffrage movement. But, since she was unavailable to the NWP as a figurehead for them, she had been reduced in stature in the pages of *Equal Rights* to "a versatile writer" little more than an assistant to Susan B. Anthony. It must have been an awkward compromise since Susan B. Anthony wasn't even at the first woman suffrage convention. Without Stanton's primary role to use in the commemorative events, a pilgrimage to Anthony's grave in Mt. Hope Cemetery in Rochester was arranged instead. With Stanton off limits and Gage's grave in Fayetteville, it left only one of the original NWSA leaders, "the triumvirate," Anthony. And, her grave was the closest to Seneca Falls."[3]

The women's movement of the 1960s and 70s reawakened an interest in women's past and the most likely starting point was the woman suffrage movement. It also, unwittingly, resurrected the contested memories of the movement. The first serious scholars of the woman suffrage movement, of course, turned to the volumes written by the participants themselves, National Woman Suffrage Association officers Stanton, Gage, and Anthony, the *History of Woman Suffrage,* Stanton's *Eighty Years and More,* and *The Life of Susan B. Anthony.* They were a tantalizing treasure trove of documents, conference resolutions, and other ephemera all compiled into well-indexed tomes. But, they were also a minefield of omissions and biases. The most notable omission from them is the scant mention of the American Woman Suffrage Association. Lucy Stone, president of the AWSA, refused to work with "those women." Had Stanton's daughter Harriet not insisted, the first three volumes would have gone to press without mentioning the sister association at all. Without actual help from the AWSA, what little there is included on it was gleaned from the pages of the AWSA newspaper, the *Woman's Journal* and a bit of subterfuge. You'll have to wait for chapter three to get the whole story on that.

While compiling the *History* letter after letter from NWSA to the state associations, Gage and Stanton cautioned that they wanted chapters focused on the work of the associations "free from personal antagonisms" and ended up encouraging a "rosy, but bland" cast to the state stories. Stanton's reminiscences never failed to reflect her enthusiasm for her own adventures; she was the star of her own show. Anthony's *Life* gave some credit where credit was due but overall conveyed the impression that Susan B. Anthony was the NWSA. Despite a recognition of their editorial slant, the abundance of these sources was perhaps a little too compelling. Even now, the majority of historical treatments are still largely about Stanton and Anthony.

Break up, Make up, Everything is Shake up!

In the case of Matilda Joslyn Gage, in the same way that political wrangling over Stanton's legacy nearly wrote her out of the memory of the suffrage past, the intrigues over the merger haunt the sources written by her adversaries in that long-ago struggle, Anthony and Stanton. The widely publicized dispute over the National Woman Suffrage Association's merger with their long-time rivals the American Woman Suffrage Association remained a sore spot with them long after the dust had settled and colored their versions of the past.

But, she couldn't be ignored completely. There was her name on the spine of the *History*, after all. And then there were over three years of the NWSA newspaper, *National Citizen and Ballot Box*, with Matilda Joslyn Gage, Editor in Chief. No, there was no way to completely ignore Gage. From her debut on the stage of her first convention in 1852, the same convention that brought Anthony into the work, she had been a close colleague with Stanton and Anthony. All this close work ended in the stormy dispute over the method, terms, and tactics the merger of NWSA and AWSA was completed. Gage left in a flurry of privately-circulated charges and counter charges that Anthony had betrayed NWSA and usurped Gage's power as Chair of the Executive Committee, that Stanton had betrayed Gage, and that Gage had betrayed them both. It got ugly. After the blowup came years of estrangement, then an uneasy truce but never again, the close companionship they had had for so many years.

Where's Matilda Joslyn Gage?

Unfortunately for Gage's place in the story of the early woman suffrage years Stanton and Anthony published the only volumes recalling the years that the three of them had been the controlling engines of the NWSA, "the triumvirate," after her death. The first three volumes of the *History of Woman Suffrage*, that they had worked on together, ended with the work up until 1885. The blowup among the three leaders came three years later. The three-volume *Life and Work of Susan B. Anthony* and *Eighty Years and More* were both published in 1898, the year Gage died. Volume IV of the *History*, covering the same ground, written by Ida Husted Harper under the direction of Anthony came out in 1902.

At the time these volumes were published, two of Gage's children wrote to Anthony objecting to the small credit their mother received, especially with regard to her work on the *HWS*. Anthony responded with a cool letter to T.C. She had always addressed letters to him with, "My dear friend." This time she addressed him as "Dear Mr. Gage" and offered a terse, "I am sorry you were pained at the omission of your mother's name by Mrs. Harper. I think she generally mentions it in connection with the history." To Gage's daughter, Helen, she wrote a more cordial, but still somewhat defensively abrupt, "My dear girl, I do not know why it was or how it was that the name of Matilda Joslyn Gage was left out of the circular (advertising the *History*) and did not notice it until your brother, Clarkson, reminded me of it; it shall certainly go back in the next (illegible) I have printed. She continues, "But in the preface to the *History* you will find full credit is given to her work on the . . . production of three chapters – 'Woman and the Newspaper' . . . 'Preceding Causes,' and 'Woman, Church and State' . . . I think you will find no other place where her name has not been mentioned, except in the circular, and I am very sorry for that, and as I say, when I get more printed I will have her name inserted."[4]

Anthony actually credits Gage with one less chapter than Harper and no changes were made in later printings. But, unlike Stanton's children, Gage's children did not attempt to set the public record right with a biography of their mother. Ironically, it may have drawn more attention to Gage if she had been left out entirely. A few anecdotes casting her as the "faithful companion" appear in the Harper volumes of the *HWS* and *The Life*. Instead, historians assumed that what Anthony/Harper/

Stanton included was all there was to include. Why look deeper when you already "know" who that Gage on the spine of three volumes of the *HWS* was?

Gage's diminished presence in the historiography of the 19th-century women's rights and woman suffrage movements is not the only loss resulting from the slanted versions written by Stanton and Harper under the direction of Anthony and followed too closely by contemporary historians.[5] The details of the merger of the two national organizations has also received surprisingly little attention. When Harper proclaimed in 1902 that the details of the merger was "not essential to the completeness" of the Anthony biography, her words should have acted like a lightning rod sparking further investigation. Instead her judgment remained conventional wisdom for much too long.

The same can be said of the documentary history of the movement. Stanton is uncritically maintained as the "matchless writer" but it is not too much to say that the work of many National women, especially Gage, has been simply credited to Stanton. If it was written, it has been assumed Stanton must have written it. With the exception of Andrea Kerr's *Lucy Stone: Speaking Out for Equality* published in 1992, nothing biographical has been published in the last decades on anyone but Stanton and Anthony. It is also surprising to find that the story of the merger, so beneficial to the American Woman Suffrage Association, gets almost no analytical coverage either.

Buried in Superlatives

During the early years of women's history research, Matilda Joslyn Gage was buried in superlatives. She was "the most logical, scientific and fearless writer of her day," according to Ida Husted Harper. She was one of the "best-known writers of the day," says Alma Lutz. Eleanor Flexner admires her for being "one of the most scholarly of them all." Wendy Martin calls her "one of the most effective and forceful woman's rights lecturers." William Leach concludes that she was "one of the most important of all nineteenth century feminist historians." Even Gage's newspaper is judged to be "a major suffrage journal" by Ellen Carol DuBois. In each instance, however, once the bouquet was thrown, Gage dropped into the background never to be heard from again.[6] She, more than any other prominent leader of the 19th-century woman's movement, was parked in an allotted niche as one of "the most" as historians hurried on to other tasks. It begs the question, if she was "the most," "the best," "effective," and "scholarly" why was she so routinely ignored? To be fair, all of these groundbreaking studies were part of the first wave of serious scholarship in the field of women's history so it's not surprising that the focus was riveted on the two best-known actors of the suffrage movement.

The problem of a still too sketchy knowledge of woman's past is a frustrating feature of all attempts to analyze a "feminist political and intellectual tradition over time." That these unsupported accolades remained unexplored for as long as they did is just another example of how shallow our understanding is of the people and events of even well-researched areas of women's history. Rather than building on the work of their predecessors, women have discovered and rediscovered that "feminist ways of thinking [have] repeatedly been interrupted and even reversed, as women, forced into ignorance of their own traditions, have had to rethink ideas their predecessors have already thought."[7]

Gage was aware of this process. Her first speech presented at the Syracuse Woman Suffrage Convention in 1852, addressed this very issue. As others described what women could do, given the chance, Gage showed how much women had already done, so much of which most women were unaware. "Our daughters" must know, "trammeled as women has been, by might and custom, there are still many shining examples, which serve as beacon lights of what may be attained by genius, labor, energy, and perseverance . . . I honor these noble women, who have been willing to pioneer in the path of duty and right . . ." For Gage, knowing woman's past was a necessary first step toward progress for women in the present. If it was said women were unfit for public life, Gage would answer, "it can be seen from Semiranis [legendary queen of Babylon] to Victoria, that she has a peculiar fitness for governing." No matter if the field be poetry, science, mathematics, astronomy, literature, or languages, Gage named scores of women in times and places past and present who had achieved greatness. Past is indeed prologue!

Although this first speech was groundbreaking, if it is mentioned, rather than being remembered for the substance of her remarks, it's remembered for her nervousness as a speaker. Good grief. Fortunately, she gained spectacular notoriety after the convention for defending the cause of women's rights and the convention from the ridicule of a local minister in the editorial columns of the *Syracuse Star.* He just had to mansplain why women's rights and the convention were ungodly. She made short work of demolishing his criticism, a story you'll enjoy reading in chapter three.

It would be the plague of her life that she was better on paper than at the podium. Try as she might, she was not the speaker that Stanton or Anthony were. But writing was her strong suit, a skill she brought to mountains of NWSA documents.[8] Among her coworkers, Gage's enthusiasm for research was legendary. Stanton remembered, "She always had a knack of rummaging through old libraries, bringing more startling fact to light than any woman I ever knew . . . From this side [her mother's] she inherited her antiquarian tastes and habits of delving into old histories, from which she has unearthed so many facts bearing on woman's degradation."[9] Another of Gage's early speeches at the 1854 Saratoga Convention impressed Judge William Hay who wrote in a letter published in Frederick Douglass's *North Star,* "Mrs. Gage, whose address was an elaborate argument for the removal of woman's legal and social disabilities cited from the same learned jurist, Wm. W. Story, laws, which had her lecture been a sermon, might have been prefixed as a text."[10]

Anthony usually admired the spirited "digging" of Gage and Stanton during the production of the *History* but was irritated by Gage's research in the situation of woman and the church, which she viewed as a waste of time. In a letter to Olympia Brown she complained, "No! We shall have but one Church and Women [referring to a proposed chapter for the *History*] and that is to be by Rev. Olympia Brown. Mrs. Gage wanted to get hers into Volume I but I have not been in favor and now it can't go in for lack of room. She has given the last two months to her church diggings and says she find things more wicked than she expected though knew its treatment of women was far from saintly. At any rate if we had room for Mrs. Gage's it wouldn't have been in the same volume with your chapter. But as I said it will be impossible for it to go in this volume." "Woman, Church and State," Chapter XV, closes Volume I.[11] The remembered years chronicled by both Stanton and Anthony have all the problems of interpretation that can be found in any type of secondary source. So, in order to locate and document Gage's actual role across the years, the primary sources are the way to go. For that the Stanton and Anthony *Papers* as well as the Gage *Papers* and the *National Citizen and Ballot Box* bring to light a much clearer picture of Gage, Stanton, Anthony, and the NWSA years.

Throughout her years in the suffrage movement Gage maintained the singular conviction that the key to woman's future was in understanding the forces that had shaped her past. With obvious disgust her friend Harriette Shattuck reported the reaction of the Executive Committee to a letter from an absent Gage to them at the 1889 NWSA Convention. "Mrs. Gage's plan of work was read at the end and received principally by laughter – the thing they laughed at was the idea of studying the philosophy of history . . . the chief thing they needed."[12] The phrase "pearls before swine" leaps to mind. Well, maybe that's too harsh. After all, not everyone had the intellectual gifts Gage had. The scope of the work of Matilda Joslyn Gage defies reduction to mere "digging and rummaging about." It is the logical, scientific, and fearless writing of this amazing woman that informs and gives substance to over forty years of suffrage documents.

NOTES

1. After considerable debate, organizers told the women that they could sit quietly in a separate women-only section curtained off from the main convention hall where they could listen to – but not participate in – the convention's proceedings. *See:* https://www.dhr.history.vt.edu/modules/us/mod04_women/evidence_detail_14.html

2. I first heard about this in 1987 at the Seventh Berkshire Conference on Women's History held at Wellesley College, in a paper delivered by Ellen Carol DuBois, "Harriot Stanton Blatch and Feminist History: Daughter to the Past." The picture is of Anita Pollitzer and Alice Paul at Anthony's grave. https://www.loc.gov/resource/mnwp.276047/

3. Stanton is buried in Woodlawn Cemetery, New York City and Gage is buried in the Fayetteville Cemetery near the site of her home in Fayetteville.

4. SBA to TCG, April 8, 1903; SBA to Helen Leslie Gage, June 16, 1903. A further omission occurs in Chapter XXV, "Trial for Voting Under Fourteenth Amendment" of *The Life*. Gage was the only nationally prominent woman who championed and defended Anthony's vote in the presidential election of 1872, canvassing Ontario Country when the trial led to a change in venue, speaking on her behalf, attending the trial, and responding to criticism in the press. This chapter acknowledges her support but is illustrated with a picture of Clemence D. Lozier. Only an autograph of Gage appears in either of the two volumes.

5. For a full discussion with copious references and scathingly brilliant remarks on the many omissions and misunderstandings by historians see, Corey, Mary E. Paddock, *Matilda Joslyn Gage: Woman Suffrage Historian, 1852-1898*, unpublished diss., University of Rochester, UMI Dissertation Services, 1995.

6. Alma Lutz, *Created Equal: a Biography of Elizabeth Cady Stanton*, (New York: John Day Co., 1940); reprinted by Octagon Books, 1974; and *Susan B. Anthony, Rebel, Crusader, Humanitarian*, (Boston: Beacon Press, 1959). Eleanor Flexner, *Century of Struggle*, (New York: Atheneum, 1970); Aileen S. Kraditor, *The Ideas of the Woman Suffrage Movement, 1890-1920*, (New York: Columbia University Press, 1965); William L. O'Neill, *Everyone Was Brave*, (Chicago: Quadrangle Books, 1971) and *True Love and Perfect Union*, (New York: Basic Books, 1980); Wendy Martin, *The American Sisterhood: Writings of the Feminist Movement from Colonial Times to the Present*, (New York: Harper & Row, 1972); Ellen Carol DuBois, *Feminism and Suffrage: The Emergence of an Independent Women's Movement in America 1848-1869*, (Ithaca: Cornell University Press, 1980) and Elizabeth Cady Stanton/Susan B. Anthony, *Correspondence, Writings, Speeches*, (New York: Schocken Books, 1981)

7. DuBois, "Introduction," Dale Spender, *Feminist Theorists, Three Centuries of Women's Intellectual Traditions* (New York: Pantheon Books, 1983) xiii.

8. *HWS*, I, 544-6, 852.

9. *Ibid.*, 466.

10. *Ibid.*, 621-2.

11. SBA to Olympia Brown, Feb. 26, 1881, *Stanton and Anthony Papers.*

12. NWSA 21 Washington Convention, Executive Committee Meeting, January 21-23, Robinson-Shattuck Papers in *Stanton and Anthony Papers.*

CHAPTER 2

Revolution to National Citizen, Gage Ink
"The Pen is Mightier than the Sword"

I F the pen was in the hand of Matilda Joslyn Gage, it was a mighty
weapon, indeed. The role of the suffrage press is a rich source of insights
into the rough and tumble of the women's movement of the 19th century.
Its role in creating and expanding a constituency for the cause has been and
continues to be ably mined by historians as well as scholars of journalism
and rhetoric. Looking to their work it is clear that the suffrage press had
a wide constellation of goals that looked to appeal to women as women.
Unlike the general circulation press that tended to limit their coverage
of women's issues to fashion, motherhood, and community service, the
suffrage press appealed to them as people, as citizens. "Creating awareness
of oppression and one's right to advocate changes for oneself, sustaining a
sense of community and purpose, identifying and answering salient issues
. . . [as well as] bridging the gaps of time and distance, educating and
uniting women across the country" were among the ambitious goals of
this special interest press.[1] Over the span of the 19th century, the woman
suffrage press helped subvert the "cult of true womanhood" and promoted
in its place "new women" fully qualified to see themselves as worthy and
necessary participants in a democracy.[2]

The importance of the woman's press was, of course, unquestioned
by the leaders of the suffrage movement themselves. The failure of the
general circulation press to appreciate or support their efforts was actually less galling than its outright hostility to them. They had to have
their own press if their conventions, speeches, meetings, and activism

were going to receive sympathetic coverage of women's changing political activities, rather than ridicule. Although the general press recognized it had a female audience, its response was an increase in coverage of "home, fashion, and etiquette" advice rather than woman's rights.

At the Saratoga Convention in 1855 Anthony urged everyone,

> "If they would be intelligent as to the real claims of the movement, they must take *The Una*. No one would expect to get temperance truths from Bennett's *Herald*, nor anti-slavery facts from the *New York Tribune* . . . no more can we look to any of the popular newspapers, political or religious for reliable information on the woman's rights movement.[3]

A number of papers sprang up and out of the moral reform-abolition temperance-women's rights agenda. Nurtured on high ideals but with low cash flow, most were short-term ventures. Woman had long associated themselves with these reform papers and supported them as best they could in an age when disposable income for woman was incredibly limited for all but the best off: upper-middle class and wealthy women, upper middle class and wealthy white women. Disposable resources for working class women and women of color were nearly non-existent and with what little they may have; a reform newspaper would not have been high on their list of priorities.[4]

Revolution!

The first "major national publication concerned solely with feminine equality" was Anthony and Stanton's own paper, *Revolution*, established in 1868. Throughout its short, stormy life, it showed the power of its vision. During the tumultuous years after the Civil War, the reform alliance between abolitionists and woman's rights advocates crumpled in the fierce infighting over suffrage priorities. For abolitionists and many woman suffragists it was "the Negro's hour" and woman suffrage would have to wait. For others, such as Stanton, Anthony, and Gage, waiting would mean losing the reform momentum of the early years of Reconstruction. Worse yet, they raged that the insertion of the word "male into the Constitution would set woman suffrage back a hundred years. So, when the first meeting of the

American Equal Rights Association after the war was held, prime on the agenda was finding some common ground within the association for the work going forward. Wendall Phillips led the meeting and essentially put it to the dissenters whether they would stand in the way of Negro suffrage. Stanton, exploded, asking Phillips ". . . do you believe the African race is composed entirely of males?"[5]

The two factions parted over irreconcilable differences. But, as a result of the split, the Stanton, Anthony, Gage faction turned to the somewhat unsavory, albeit wealthy financier, George Francis Train. True, he was in favor of woman suffrage but, oh my, his other stances should have given them pause. He was rabidly anti-Negro and a Democrat, when being a Democrat in the South came with a truckload of baggage. His support offered one overarching consideration that put all other concerns on the furthest back burner – he had the money to make it possible for them to publish their newspaper. Anthony, especially, had been eager to publish a newspaper of their own within moments after joining the cause. Train's money came with a certain stench, but it was a stench they could handle as long as it meant another issue of *Revolution* rolled off the press. It seemed like quite a deal. Train required no ideological compromise from them and his only stipulation was that they leave room for him to publish his financial advice column.[6]

From its first issue *Revolution* provoked heated rebukes from enemies and allies alike. The first issue, January 8, 1868, proved it was not going to shy away from the issues of the day that most impacted women. Its style was smart, aggressive, and inflammatory. No one was surprised to find the fiercest rebukes from William Lloyd Garrison, Lucy Stone, and Henry Brown Blackwell, former allies turned harshest critics. The final rupture between them came at the May 1865 AERA[7] Convention. A brief foray into the minutes will show what I mean. First, Frederick Douglass led a contingent that supported a resolution in favor of the passage of the proposed Fifteenth Amendment enfranchising black men to vote and excluding all women, black and white. Stephen Foster supported him and the two called for the resignations of Anthony and Stanton. Ernestine Rose and Josephine Griffing ignored Douglass and Foster's proposal and instead offered their proposal that the association change its name from the American Equal Rights Association to the Woman Suffrage Association. Clearly there was no possibility of containing either the disparity of purpose between suffrage priorities or the outright hostility among the members within the confines of the association. They simply didn't care to be associated with each other any longer. This, then, was the swan song of the old AERA.

Birth of the National

Two days after the final adjournment of the now defunct AERA convention, the editors of *Revolution* hosted a reception for women delegates at their New York City office. As they explained it later, the reception with barely a ripple in the waters, segued into an organizing meeting. And, just like that the National Woman Suffrage Association was born. These women had been organizing associations all their lives, so organizing was second nature to them and for this association, the goals were very simple. First: A commitment to a Sixteenth Amendment explicitly establishing woman suffrage in the Constitution. Second: Theirs would be an association controlled and defined by women. That's right – no boys allowed. When they were done Elizabeth Cady Stanton was the new president, Susan B. Anthony was the new Chair of the Executive Committee, and Matilda Joslyn Gage Chair of the Advisory Committee. Conspicuously absent from the meeting were Lucy Stone and Henry Blackwell. Blackwell charged the organizer with deliberately keeping their intention to form a woman suffrage association from them so that they would not stay in New York long enough to attend. Well, yes, they did but they were understandably reluctant to say so in so many words. Instead they published Celia Burleigh's version of the proceedings in the *Revolution*. In that version "A spontaneous, unanimous sentiment among the women delegates erupted to form their own association." Blackwell and Stone were convinced otherwise.[8]

Counter Revolution: The American is Born

Still smarting from the events of the May convention, its aftermath and continued criticism in the pages of the *Revolution*, the New England suffragists formed their own association, the American Woman Suffrage Association, the following November. The creation of the second woman suffrage association roused ambivalent reactions on the part of many suffragists and especially from Susan B. Anthony. Her curiosity piqued, she attended the new association's November convention as a spectator and, when voted out of the audience and onto the platform, gave a short speech declaring, ". . . to be glad for the convention even if it should cancel the National and the *Revolution,* so long as it secures votes for women."[9] In the December 9, 1869, edition of the *Revolution,* however, Anthony instructed members now featured among lists of proposed AWSA officers, "You must decide for yourself . . . I cannot advise you one way or the other." A statement followed reiterating that "all who argue for woman's freedom are with me" but she then changed her stance to question whether the real aim of the AWSA "is woman's suffrage or to count out Mrs. Stanton, Susan B. Anthony, and ignore the *Revolution.*" She concluded the article, however, with "earnest hope that all are melded into one at the (NWSA) anniversary meeting in May."[10] The January 6, 1870, issue again revealed a desire for reconciliation. In a short article describing the upcoming Washington Convention the Committee on Arrangements expressed its hope ". . . that the leaders of AWSA, Lucy Stone, Mary A. Livermore, Julia Ward Howe, and other 'cross overs' will attend."[11] The January 13 issue continued this pattern and enthusiastically congratulated the newest arrival on the suffrage newspaper scene, Stone and Blackwell's *The Woman's Journal.* But it seems very possible that Anthony realized that there were not enough suffragists to support two national papers, because this issue also has a tiny article with the silly headline, "Don't Know Its Mother!" encouraging the readers of the *Revolution* to subscribe to all the "children" it had spawned:

The Woman's Advocate (Ohio)

The Woman's Advocate (New York)

The Agitator (Chicago)

The Woman's Journal (Boston)[12]

More bad news arrived with the notice that Train would no longer continue his financial backing as of May, 1869. So, by January, 1870 the *Revolution* was in trouble. Its low subscription rate, $3 per year, and its small number of subscribers, about 3,000, took their toll as debts mounted. Between January and May 1879 when the paper was sold,

Anthony briefly entertained the possibility of accepting the financial support of Harriet Beecher Stowe and Isabella Beecher Hooker, through the creation of a stock company. It would have relieved her of all financial responsibility by making her simply the business manager. The Beecher sisters, however, required that she change the name of the paper to something less radical like *The True Republic*. It was a tempting offer but in the end Stanton and others convinced her that the change would probably kill the paper anyway. *The Revolution* limped along until May when it was sold to Laura Curtis Bullard for the token fee of one dollar. As Anthony put it, she felt like, "a mother binding out a dear child she can't support." She was left with only the paper's $10,000 debt.[13]

The Woman's Journal had a much smoother start. It began on firm financial footing in January 1870 and would become the longest-lived publication of the suffrage press, publishing until 1932. Lucy Stone and Henry Browne Blackwell began publishing it under the auspices of the AWSA and were joined by Mary A. Livermore, merging her Chicago-based paper, the *Agitator* with the *Journal* and taking on the role of editor. Thus, two of *The Revolution*'s "children" not only knew but slew their mother.[14]

The impact of the *Revolution* on the suffrage struggle has been ably described by Campbell, Dow, and Masel-Walters and recent scholarship has not challenged their findings. In terms of its function as a catalyst to the division of the movement into two separate organizations, its focus on woman suffrage on equal terms with black male suffrage, its iconoclastic discussions of important women's issues and its education of middle-class women, the *Revolution* set the standard for all the suffrage publications that would follow.[15] One impact of the *Revolution* that's received less attention, however, is its use as a forum for suffrage activists like Matilda Joslyn Gage. One could get the impression that the whole of the *Revolution* was written by Anthony and Stanton, but that was not the case. The *Revolution* can also claim its role as a showcase for women who would become stalwarts of the movement, especially Matilda Joslyn Gage, who brought to the *Revolution* an established reputation as a writer.

Writing for the *Revolution*

Gage was already well known in reform circles as both a writer and speaker when she became a regular contributor to the *Revolution*.[16] In her first article for the April 9, 1868, edition she addressed "Susan" affectionately to express her best wishes for the success of the paper, and recalled the Saratoga Convention of 1854 when she, Susan and Sarah Pellet were the only speakers. The main topic of the article, however, was her reply to an article on "child murder" and an argument in favor of woman's right to her person. Concluding, she offers to ". . . write occasionally if health and eyes permit." She was apparently blessed with very good health and eyes as she remained a monthly, sometimes semi-monthly contributor for the duration of the paper. Among her articles was a six-installment series entitled "Woman as Inventor" that ran from April, 1868 to October, 1869; Woman's Right to Her Own Person;" and several articles on the problems of women teachers. Notices of her speaking tours and her reports from the field while on tour also appeared.[17]

May, 1869, marked the beginning of the split in the AERA and brought Stanton, Anthony, and Gage as well as the *Revolution* into direct conflict with the rest of their colleagues with the formation of the NWSA. From that point on Gage's articles were less personally inspired and more frequently submitted on behalf of the NWSA or the New York State Woman Suffrage Association. As an officer in both of these associations, Gage's articles reflected her activities organizing local associations and conducting county conventions. Reports of conventions held, resolutions adopted, and speeches scheduled became the more usual submissions. By the November and December issues, 1869, the paper fairly bristled with the news of the upcoming Washington Convention slated for January, 18 and 19, 1870.[18] From the tone of the articles in the early months of 1870 it would have been hard to foresee the *Revolution's* demise less than six months later.

Beginning with her first convention in 1852, through the war years and the organization of NWSA and continuing through the *Revolution*-ary years, Gage moved quickly to the forefront of the woman suffrage movement and into leadership positions. Along with Stanton and

Anthony, she was elected to and continued to hold high offices in the NWSA. Between 1870 and 1890 she was at various times Chair of the Executive Committee, Chair of the Committee on Resolutions, Corresponding Secretary, Vice-president, or President. Unlike Stanton who needed continual prodding to get her to attend conventions, Gage rarely missed a meeting and was notably associated with NWSA's most public demonstrations: Anthony's trial for voting in 1872, the Woman's Declaration at the Centennial Celebration in Philadelphia in 1876, and the Rochester Resolutions presented at the Anniversary Convention in 1878 that raised such a storm in pulpits and press. Clearly, she was primed for an even larger public presence.[19]

Without the *Revolution*, NWSA no longer had a paper of its own and was forced to publish its convention calls in whatever suffrage papers that were available. They even had to resort to the general circulation press at times. They also had to rely on these outlets to report on the proceedings of their conventions with mixed results. Another paper was desperately needed, one that they could control and upon which they could rely for maximum visibility and complete coverage. Nothing was so frustrating than submitting detailed documentation of their work only to find an abbreviated version appearing in these alternative outlets.

One paper that was most careful with their materials was the paper owned by Sarah R. L. Williams, *The Ballot Box*, and publishing on behalf of the Toledo Woman Suffrage Association. It had begun publishing in 1876 with a shaky foundation. As Williams noted in that first edition,

"In launching our little bark upon the uncertain sea of public favor, we feel that we are acting under a positive want which exists in the community, and that our call to do so is sufficiently urgent to justify the venture."

Although a local paper, its pages were soon filled with news from the National. Especially exciting was the upcoming Philadelphia Centennial Celebration in July and plans for NWSA's participation. At this time Gage had just stepped down as President of NWSA and had just been elected to Chair of the Executive Committee; Stanton was once again elected President, and Anthony was sharing Corresponding Secretary duties with Sarah J. Spencer and Jane Graham Jones. *The Ballot Box* for June and July could have been mistaken for the official NWSA paper, so much so that it was no surprise when in August Elizabeth Cady Stanton wrote to Williams,

> "We have decided, in the Executive Committee, to make *The Ballot Box* the organ of the National Woman Suffrage Association, and we shall do all in our power to keep you well informed of what is done, and to extend your circulation. I believe Miss Anthony has already sent you her list of subscribers to the *Revolution,* and Mrs. Gage a report of our last most successful meeting in Philadelphia."[20]

This same August issue also contained the first announcement of the proposed history by Stanton, Anthony, and Gage along with a notice asking supporters to write "their full name and their state, (nothing else) on a *thin* slip of paper and send to Matilda Joslyn Gage, Fayetteville, N. Y." in order that their autographs could be affixed in the official NWSA Autograph Album. Successive issues continued to devote much of its space to NWSA news, letters, and articles from the NWSA officers. Williams published *The Ballot Box* for another two years before ill health made it impossible for her to go on. The thought of losing yet another outlet for their work was so disappointing. It was then that, on behalf of NWSA, Gage purchased it and moved it to her home in Fayetteville. Huzzah! The National would again, after eight long years, have a paper of its own.

No Stranger to Publishing

Gage was supremely suited to the task of editing and publishing. Her roots in both reform movements and the reform press were strong and deep. Her parents were both ardent supporters of abolition and their home was frequently used for meetings of the Central New York abolitionists and as a stop on the underground railroad. They also supported the temperance cause and her father published *The State League,* the newspaper of the New York temperance association, the Carson League, from its formation until his death in 1865. Gage, herself, was well known locally as a writer long before her entry in woman suffrage work. Her serial romance, "The Heiress and

Her Cousin," a tale of mistaken identities and unrequited love, percolated through six installments of the Skaneateles [New York] *Democrat* in 1851. "The Stranger in Black," a mystery-romance in three parts entertained the readers of her hometown paper, the Fayetteville *Recorder* in part because of its local setting. *The Central New Yorker, The Syracuse Journal* and other local papers were home to her lively travelogues. Vacations and speaking engagements around the state occasioned wonderfully detailed pieces on the sights, sounds, foods, and history of such exotic locales as Niagara Falls, Saratoga Springs, Ballston Spa, and her own Fayetteville-Manlius area. At a time when even a trip from Fayetteville to Niagara Falls was beyond the reach of many, these travelogues did then what *Rick Steves Europe* does for us today – took the arm chair traveler on an adventure to parts unknown and showed them places they may never see but could dream about. Even after becoming fully involved with suffrage work, she continued to send home her travel pieces, now with a woman's rights slant, from Washington, New York City, Philadelphia, Boston and beyond; wherever her speeches were needed or conventions were held.

One of the first clippings in her scrapbook, "Ionetta: The Tale of a Great Heroine, Founded on Historical Fact," published under her pen name, "Ande-Coral," shows her early interest in the achievements of women. Her unique perspective that women had already gone and done and achieved great things set her apart from other women reformers of her day. While others eagerly anticipated what women could do, once their rights had been secured, Gage focused on how much they had already accomplished to prove that women in other times and places had showed courage, intellect, and outstanding abilities. For her, it was not women who must change; they were already capable of the most challenging deeds. No, for her, it was society that must change. It must remove its foot from her neck. "Ionetta," she wrote, "was a Greek maiden living in Nicasia at the time of its invasion by the Ottoman Turks. With the city in ruins and 25,000 of the vanquished facing life in bondage, she and her companions were secured on a ship bound for the sultan's harem. Preferring death to dishonor, Ionetta formulated a plan to destroy the ship. "They found means to fire the magazine, which caused the destruction of the ship, themselves, and the Turks.

This act . . . was at once their death and their monument: a monument of courage and virtue."[21] More important than it dubious conclusion, is its evidence of Gage's innate understanding that women needed "great women." Written about 1853, it was one of the first of her many essays on great women of the past. No one in the woman suffrage movement had a better command of woman's changing situation over time than Gage. What women lacked, she felt, was not great women and accomplishments great and small by women throughout history on which to ground their future, but education to claim this "usable past." Women knew so little about women. Without the words for the concept, Gage was a lifelong advocate of women's studies.

Scrapping with Sunderland

A practical use for her accumulating insights into woman's past appeared shortly after the Syracuse Woman's Rights Convention of 1852, Gage's first. In response to the heresy of women's rights, "A Sermon on Women's Rights" by Rev. Byron Sunderland was published in the *Syracuse Star,* a pro-slavery newspaper. Sunderland dredged up an obscure reference from the Mosaic Code, Deut. 22:5, to begin mansplaining the errors of the very idea of women's rights and to ridicule in particular the few brave women wearing the "Bloomer" costume. "The woman shall not wear that which pertaineth unto a man; neither shall a man put on a woman's garment; for all that do are an abomination to the Lord thy God." To his chagrin, instead of effectively discrediting the convention, he found himself skewered with his own sources and filleted by the erudition and wit of Gage.

Using the same Mosaic laws, Gage wrote a review of the sermon, asking to know why he,

". . . being one of the priesthood does not minister in a robe whose hem is trimmed with bells of gold, neither does he wear a bonnet of fine linen, still less regard does he pay to the Mosaic sanctity of the seventh day as recorded, Ex. 35:2, 3, but . . . preaches on the first day of the week. Neither does he deem it incumbent to command his flock to heed the laws recorded, Deut. 22: 6, ll, 12, but stop, I may err . . . But even excluding this last, I think we have sufficiently demonstrated that 'the folks of progress nowadays' include the learned divine among their number."

Her review of his other arguments pointed out their internal inconsistencies and Sunderland's selective use of Old Testament exhortations if and when they suited his purposes. In one argument he says "woman has the privilege of an intelligent, responsible and moral being within her appropriate sphere . . ." In another he "states man is the representative of the woman, and that she has no right to say anything within the limits of the marriage vow, without his permission, because he becomes responsible for her act." But, what else would you expect Gage asked, from "an upholder of American slavery, in which institution the master cast votes both for himself and his slaves."

She also criticized his literary style. Dripping with sarcasm she wrote, "The sublime phraseology occasionally used by the learned divine deserves notice for it classic beauty and causes his to rank second to none in pulpit oratory. Who will attempt to vie in rhetorical eloquence and purity of expression with the 'example to youth' given in this passage, 'placing a woman and a man alternately on the back of the donkey of public affairs, and causing the two elements of humanity to go hipty hop on the journey of time.' Shad of Masillon draw near!"

Sunderland was obviously stunned by the unsigned review but complained about the "errors" in it. Therefore, if the author "should turn out to be a man I should have no objection to point out these inaccuracies through your columns. But if the writer is a lady why I really don't know yet what I shall do. If I thought she would consent to a personal interview, I should like to see her." The following week the general public chimed in and protested his logic on the editorial page. "How's this? The dominie appealed to Scripture and the Reviewer has him fast. Are we to understand that it is an article in Anti-Progressive Ethics that the same article written by a man, will be answered by Mr. Sunderland, but written by a woman, will not be answered?" So challenged, Sunderland could do nothing else but reply. However, he had backed himself into a theological corner again and was again bested by Gage signing with her well-known "M." In the end, Sunderland was:

". . . obliged to entrench himself behind these two positions:

1. That the Levitical law is all abrogated except that part of it relating to dress.

2. That Deborah, the Judge of Israel, was not a ruler in Israel.

"On these two points she may well leave her antagonist and let him spit his fury at her . . . Hers is an unimpassioned, logical, truthful argument. His is a concatenation of falsities, quibbles, and black-guard."[22]

In the same way that the ruling race had tried to limit and interpret the Bible to keep slaves docile and obedient, the ruling sex used Scripture to dominate women. It was something new, however, to have an educated woman turn scripture into a tool, to expose that clerical strategy, and do it on behalf of her own liberation. From this first resounding thump, Gage came to be known for her unimpassioned, logical arguments on behalf of women's rights.

The National Citizen and Ballot Box

If there was any question about the value of the new addition to the suf-frage ranks, Gage demonstrated in this exchange that she was an able advocate. From her first convention, in both her prepared speeches and her debate with Sunderland, she proved herself a force to be reckoned with as a scholar and historian of women's history. These were the skills Gage sup-plied throughout her association with Anthony, Stanton, and the National. In 1878, after twenty-six years of suffrage work, she was no stranger to publishing or to the public when she bought *The Ballot Box* and brought it to national attention. In her farewell column, Mrs. Williams, editor and owner, wrote, "Mrs. Gage's faithful labors in behalf of woman's equality before the law are too well known to the readers of *The Ballot Box* and to the public generally, to need any rehearsal on our part."[23]

Unlike *Revolution, The National Citizen and Ballot Box* was not born in controversy. By taking over the work of Sarah Williams' paper, it arrived on the scene with a small change in its title and the good will of all its former subscribers and the subscriber lists Anthony had left over from *Revolution*. And, since Williams' paper had already given over most of its space to NWSA news, it was an easy transition to becoming the official newspaper of NWSA. Gage changed the name of the paper as soon as she bought it, much to Anthony's consternation. Stanton, on the other hand, was delighted with it. In "appearance and name, [it] so well represents our purpose and association." Whereas Anthony didn't like the addition of "national citizen" to the name, Stanton said she would, "drop the "ballot box . . ."24 So, with about as much consensus as these three opinionated women ever reached, the project was launched. Gage was owner and editor and publisher. Anthony and Stanton appeared on the masthead as "corresponding editors." What is surprising about the launch of the paper is its timing. Such was the urgency to have their own newspaper again, they agree to start it at the same time as they began work on what would become Volume I of *History of Woman Suffrage.* Of course, when they first began working on the history, they had no way of knowing that what they saw as putting together a booklet would become three octavo volumes. At the time it probably seemed like an opportune time. All three were already regularly doing speaking tours and providing NWSA news to *The Ballot Box.* Ever since the loss of *The Revolution,* Anthony especially had hoped to have another paper and Gage was familiar with the nuts and bolts of newspaper publishing and needed an income. How could they resist rescuing a suffrage paper on the verge of closing that was already closely identified with NWSA? They couldn't. It was too good an opportunity to let it slip by them.25

May, 1878, saw the first issue of the *NCBB.* In many ways it maximized the fact that readers had been accustomed to *The Ballot Box,* so, Gage wisely retained the four-page, five-column format. Three and a half pages were devoted to NWSA and other suffrage news with one-half page set aside for advertisements. Most readers were subscribers at one dollar a year, including postage, but at least one Syracuse newsstand, Mosher's New and Used Books, sold it at ten cents a copy. It was printed by Masters and Stone of Syracuse. Gage inherited about two thousand subscribers from Williams and quickly began advertising for new subscriptions. As mentioned before, Gage bought the paper because she needed an income. So, it's no surprise to see in the first edition a tastefully headed notice designed to catch the attention of subscribers in arrears: PAY UP! It would appear that along with about two thousand subscribers she also inherited an unspecified number of subscribers behind in their payments.

For this paper, as is true of most small presses, money was an on-going concern, which accounts for periodic reminders to renew subscriptions and pay in full. Anthony's major contribution to the *NCBB* was her tireless work soliciting subscriptions, just as she had for *The Ballot Box*. At lectures, at conventions, and in most correspondence she urged all who supported woman suffrage to buy a subscription and " . . . thus help our cause on."26

Another way small newspapers stayed solvent was through a practice called clubbing. The February, 1879 issue offered clubbed subscriptions with eleven other publications. Clubbing allowed subscribers the advantage of two or more journals at reduced prices, usually a standard 20 percent discount. The *NCBB* offered to club with *The Woman's Journal, The Women's Tribune, Woman's Words, The Alpha, The Weekly Inter-Ocean, The Housekeeper, The Woman's Exponent, Appleton's Journal, Popular Science Monthly, North American Review,* and *The New York Medical Journal.*27 It was, of course, a device to increase circulation and income. It was also a way to let subscribers of other like-minded publications that your publication was available. This was especially important for new papers or papers under new management.

Gage found that Lucy Stone drove a hard bargain to club with her *Woman's Journal.* Due to the difference in size and frequency of publication between the two papers. Gage initially offered Stone a club price of only seventy-five cents a year but Stone wrote back that she thought five copies of the *National Citizen* for every one copy of the *WJ* was a more reasonable exchange because the *WJ* "offered more reading matter than yours [Gage's]."28 Although Gage was not happy with Stone's terms, she agreed to them to secure Stone's cooperation for the Massachusetts section of the *History.* Earlier in the month she had written to Stone hoping to get her help, "As my desire is to do justice to all the early workers, I shall be glad, as will my associates, of any facts, etc. that either yourself or others may give us . . . A sketch of your own life and work, also Mr. Blackwell's, the history of Massachusetts and of the American Association will be gladly received. All such aid will be eventually acknowledged.[29] As it turned out, Stone got great terms but never did cooperate on the *History*.

Premiums were also offered to pique enthusiasm. In order to increase circulation, woman's rights tracts, pictures of Lucretia Mott, and copies of volume one were offered as a freebie with ten subscriptions. It worked. Based on Anthony's figures, circulation reached approximately 4,300 by the end of 1880.[30] The *NCBB* also supported itself by selling advertising space. Rates in 1878, the only year rates were published in the paper itself were:

Per square-nine lines nonpareil squares ¾ inch		One-fourth column 5 ½"	
One month	$ .50	One month	$ 2.50
Two	.90	Two	4.00
Three	1.30	Three	5.00
Four	1.70	Six	9.00
Five	2.00	One year	16.50
Six	2.25		
One year	4.00		

Other rates for larger ads were proportionately higher, $30 for a half column for one year and $50 for a full column ad for a year. These rates were comparable to those of other newspapers of the time.[31]

One of the things Gage did not inherit from the *Ballot Box* was an advertising base. Mrs. Williams advertisers were all local to the Ohio area. Gage followed that path and all but two of her advertisers were either local, Syracuse area businesses and professionals or lecturers, journals, or professionals associated with woman suffrage. Attorney Belva Lockwood's and Dr. Caroline B. Winslow's, *The Alpha*, published by the Moral Education Society of Washington, D. C., regularly advertised in the *NCBB*. One advertiser that did make the transition from *The Ballot Box* was the very popular *Buckeye Cookery and Practical Housekeeping*. They ran a half column advertisement for door-to-door saleswomen for eight months, from October, 1878, to May, 1879. "PAYING WORK! For Refined Women" The ad continued, "Hundreds of Refined and

Cultivated Women need open air work that pays liberally and is congenial." Published out of Marysville, Ohio, it was "so practical and so attractive to women, (especially housekeepers) it practically sold itself." And, its second edition featured Elizabeth Cady Stanton's, "Something About Babies."[32] The only other cross-over advertiser was Peter Henderson & Co., a mail order garden supplier selling "Everything for the Garden" from 35 Cortland Street, New York, New York. This ad, however, only ran twice in June and July, 1878.

A Shift in the Advertisers

Actually, all this information about advertising rates and what ads crossed over is pretty dry stuff until you see what happened in the advertising pages at the end of the first year. An interesting transition began. Local advertising started to dwindle but NWSA advertising soared. By February, 1880, the only local advertiser, Kent & Miller Clothing, remained. A few months later McCarthy's Fabrics made a 3-month encore appearance but after that, almost no strictly local ads were placed in the *NCBB*. As its reputation as a national newspaper grew so did the advertising from more national businesses such as Talbot's Temperance Hotel, offers of NWSA tracts and pictures of NWSA leaders, Woman Suffrage Photographs, The Women's National Lyceum Bureau, Clemence S. Lozier's University of the State of New York Medical College and Hospital for Women, Spencerian Business College, Sara A. Spencer, Vice-principal, Eva L. Finney's Lectures, Hotel Burns of Syracuse. Want ads looked for agents to sell the *History of Woman Suffrage* and ads for Gage's own lectures. This kind of transition from local to national advertising didn't happen for *The Ballot Box*. In spite of its clearer identification with the NWSA during its last year, it kept its identity as a Toledo newspaper and kept its local advertisers. Just the opposite was the case with the *NCBB*. From its first edition it positioned itself as an explicitly national woman suffrage paper and its advertisers became more explicitly tied to woman suffrage.

In spite of all the efforts to secure advertisements, advertising must have played only a minor part in the financial structure of the paper. Even at the start it only set aside one-half page for advertising. "Most papers of the era devoted more than one-half of available space to advertising, some as much as four-fifths and nine-tenths. Political papers were often three-quarters advertisements. Advertising was the usual way to keep a newspaper afloat since subscription rates were really low. What does stand out is the importance of subscribers. For the *NCBB* subscriptions were gathered by paid canvassers but the bulk of new subscriptions came from Anthony's work. Everywhere Anthony spoke and in every letter she wrote she included a reminder to subscribe to the *NCBB*. When Anthony took time away from the lecture circuit at the end of 1880 to devote her energies to getting a publisher for the *HWS*, Gage was clearly worried and at that point considered giving up the paper. Of course, as soon as Anthony heard about Gage's concerns, she immediately wrote a confidential letter to Rachel Foster describing Gage's situation. ". . . she has no money and she dares run no risk whatever . . . The paper has little more than paid its way." Perhaps Rachel could take the paper to Philadelphia should Gage be forced to give it up. Anthony had already begun courting wealthy women to the cause and apparently had no problem sharing personal information about Gage with a newcomer if she could save the paper. Some friend. Rachel, for her part, buoyed by Anthony's championing of her ahead of Gage, became a ready participant in several other of Anthony's little disloyalties, (See Chapter four, Union/Disunion) this time with far-reaching consequences.

To Make Those Women Discontented!

As it turned out, losing Anthony's subscription work did result in a loss of $700 to $800 that year, but Gage did manage to publish it for another year. The paper's philosophy was explicitly stated in the Prospectus: it's intention was to

> "advocate the principle that suffrage is a citizen's right and should be protected by national law and while states may regulate the suffrage, they should have no power to abolish it."[33]

Although the NWSA's 1878 Tenth Washington Convention officially decided to pursue woman suffrage via a constitutional amendment and abandoned the strategy of taking their case to the courts claiming the right to vote under the Fourteenth Amendment's definition of national citizenship and its guarantee of equal protection, Gage continued to defend proceeding through the courts but saw the virtue in pursuing a constitutional amendment as well. She set high goals for the paper. Its purpose was

> . . . to secure national protection to women citizens in the exercise of their right to vote;

> but it will also touch upon the woman question in all its various aspects: it proposes a general criticism of men and things.

> Neither fear not favor will hinder its presentation of truth and the calling of attention to unjust customs and laws; it will oppose class legislation of whatever form.

> It will support no political party until one arises which is based upon the exact permanent political equality of men and women.

> As the first process towards becoming well is to know that you are ill, one of the principal aims of the NATIONAL CITIZEN is to make those women discontented who are now content – to waken them to self respect, and a desire to use the talents they may possess – to educate their consciences aright to quicken their sense of duty – to destroy morbid beliefs and make them worthy of the life with which their creator has endowed them.[34]

Its purpose was to do no less than to "revolutionize the country, striving to make it live up to its own fundamental principles and become in reality what it is but in name – a Republic."[35] It would be published monthly and would be the official exponent of the views and positions of the National Woman Suffrage Association. Of course, there was some push back to her goals as stated. In general, the response to the new paper was enthusiastic but some were uncomfortable with its forthright goal "to make those women discontented who are now content." Mercy, Maude, get my smelling salts! *The Fayetteville Recorder, The Desert Evening News* (Salt Lake City), *The Vineland Times,* and the *Geneva Times* (New York) all howled in protest. The language was "too bitter against men!" Gage was having none of it. Over the next few months she shot back: "No blow is ever struck until discontent is felt. Mrs. Stanton [agrees but] takes the entirely opposite view of the question and argues that every woman is *now* in a state of chronic discontent."[36]

The paper itself was organized under seven broad headings: NWSA news, national politics, New York politics, Gage's editorials, columnists, foreign news, and consciousness raising. Of the seven categories, NWSA news always commanded the front page. Calls to conventions, local, regional, and national; reports of testimony before Senate and House committees, convention minutes and speeches; NWSA financial reports; elections of officers; and sample petition forms all found space on the front page. As Corresponding Editors, the front page also made room for letters from Miss Anthony and Mrs. Stanton. Convention reports were especially important. Most women hungry for NWSA news couldn't leave children and their households to travel to New York City or Washington, D.C. Stanton often lamented, "Women are paupers" and the financial burden of traveling to conventions were prohibitive. The *NCBB* filled the void and provided women across the country with a sense of being a part of the action. Each session was described in great detail and most speeches printed in their entirety – or at least the best parts. Some of the speakers were especially popular. Lillie Devereux Blake was noted for her biting sense of humor so her speeches were eagerly awaited. Folks looked forward to yet another iteration of the Smith sisters "Why We Didn't Pay Our Taxes." It was good to know that the Henderson Family Singers had been at the convention to bring their brand of political protests in song. And, of course, everyone wanted to know who the new officers were. From the length of the lists, there was an office for everyone committed to the cause. Lists of delegates and officers familiarized women living far from Washington and New York with both the national leaders and like-minded women in their own neck of the woods.[37]

Anthony and Gage seldom missed conventions and commanded prime speaking slots, so their speeches were always eagerly awaited by subscribers. And, when Stanton could not, or would not attend, she always sent a letter to be read into the record on her behalf. The Washington conventions filled the paper with arguments presented before

Congressional committees. For women living far from the capital with its centers of power it must have been exhilarating to read that some women were being respectfully received in the halls of government.

Beginning with the September, 1878, issue the most important front page columns were enticing excerpts from NWSA's latest project: the – *History of Woman Suffrage.* "For the purpose of thus perfecting the *History,* Gage first presented it in newspaper form."[38] Each month approximately three of its five front page columns were given over to the first chapters of the *History,* beginning with Gage's own, "Preceding Causes." The last installments before going to press with Volume I, "Women Under Christianity" by Gage and her tribute to Lucretia Mott written by Gage and Stanton, appeared in the February, 1881, issue. The installments were more than just an attempt to promote the eventual publication in book form. It was also an attempt to solicit corrections and additions from the readership before it went to press. The *History* began in her newspaper and later the *NCBB* provided the bulk of material that became the first third of Volume III, covering 1876–1883.[39]

Political Action

One of the reasons NWSA held its conventions in Washington each year while Congress was in session was to establish itself as a presence in national politics. Therefore, national politics was an important part of the news in the *NCBB.* Between 1878 and 1881 NWSA and the *NCBB* closely followed the progress of the Lockwood Bill, the Sixteenth Amendment, and presidential campaign of 1880. The *NCBB* carried both the arguments of their opponents and their rebuttals to them. They published lists of their prime targets: Senators Wadleigh of New Hampshire; McMillan of Minnesota; Ingals of Kansas; Saulsbury of Delaware; Merriman of North Carolina; and Hill of Georgia. All had opposed their proposed suffrage amendment in the Senate Committee on Privileges and Elections and received appropriate heat from NWSA in the *NCBB.* And, not to allow complacency, friends were taken to task when necessary. "Where," the *NCBB* wanted to know, "were Senators Hoar, Mitchell and Cameron? Asleep, that they were not ready with their minority report to offset Wadleigh's adverse one? Were all suffrage friends 'out' even Senator Sargent?"[40]

A happier outcome came with the passage of the Lockwood Bill. It allowed "any woman, a member in good standing of the highest court in any state or territory, or of the Supreme Court of the District of Columbia for three years be admitted to practice in the United States Supreme Court. It passed the Senate February 7, 1879. By signature of President Hayes and the motion of Hon. A. G. Riddle on March 3, Belva Lockwood was admitted to the bar of the Supreme Court of the United States. This time Senators Hoar, Sargent, and MacDonald received large baskets of flowers for their hard work on behalf of women from the NWSA.[41] Gage's editorial, February, 1878, included a full list of senators voting for and against the bill identified by political party, "Republicans in Roman characters, Democrats in italics . . . and noted that their old nemesis "Wadleigh now votes in the affirmative."

The presidential election of 1880 and how the outcome might affect woman suffrage for the foreseeable future was the most important story of that year in terms of space in the paper. It was a disappointing year but offers testimony to the expanded political role women had assumed long before suffrage itself was achieved. As early as February readers were told not to waste time or energy on the Greenbackers. "Independently of the fact that no small third party is worth spending time upon . . . the Greenbackers have proven themselves especially treacherous."[42] An invitation to "suffrage reformers" to support them was removed from its published list of supporters and a letter for publication from E. M. Davis, an active member of the Greenbackers, later confirmed that the party was now being led by one, Mr. Delamatyr, "who was not to be trusted."[43]

In spite of Davis's letter NWSA planned a mass meeting in Chicago to impress through strength of numbers both the Republicans and the Greenbackers. Both parties were meeting in Chicago and NWSA wanted their numbers to impress on both parties the need to include woman suffrage in their platforms. The Republicans were especially disappointing and denied them "even the splinters of '72 and '76." Anthony was invited to address the Resolutions Committee but was held to a ten-minute time limit and was quickly ushered out by the Chair, Edward Pierrepont when her time was up. No resolution in favor of woman suffrage could have been expected from this committee that made clear its hostility to it and none was received.[44]

Many suffragists held higher hopes for positive results at the Greenback convention. They were rebuffed there too. *NWSA* attempts to address this convention were met with hoots and hisses from the members and here too they were forced to leave a convention empty handed. July's edition summarized the positions of all four candidates based on their letters of acceptance of the nominations of their respective parties. Garfield made no mention of woman suffrage, and in a personal interview with Anthony said he was 'not convinced." Gage editorialized that "We are 'not convinced' that he is fit to be President." J.B. Weaver was thought to be a woman suffragist but does not mention it either. The Prohibition Party candidate, Neal Dow included woman suffrage in his letter and the Party included a strong woman suffrage plank but had, "too little present political influence to make it best for women." And as for the Democrats, "General Hancock, lacking either time or brains, will not have his letter ready in a fortnight yet, but being a species of political prophet, we need not wait to see it. We can rest assured that if the two candidates who have been called suffragists made no mention of woman suffrage, neither will the man who refused Mrs. Surratt's pleading daughter the privilege of seeing her mother the night before her execution."[45]

NWSA decided that since they weren't getting anything from the major candidates and the only strong endorsement came from the Prohibition Party, a party of minimal consequence in a presidential race, they wouldn't endorse anyone. The full measure of their frustration can be seen in Gage's editorial, "Professed Friends." Here she answers criticism of NWSAs appeal to all the candidates for their support of woman suffrage and their decision not to endorse any candidate, even the Republicans. The *Women's Journal,* attempted to scold them saying ". . . the primary object of government is to govern." She shot back with ". . . this is an idea fit only for autocratic Russia." Anthony, with even less patience for the rival paper had this to say after reading its various ". . . criticisms and flings, [I] must say they are in the main very weak, if not wicked." In "Woman Idolators" Gage took aim a second time and delivered a blast to women who still idolized the Republican Party.

"Open your eyes, women. Use common sense. Look at your position as it is. Examine the past of the Republican Party in regard to women and having found your idol made of clay, break it to pieces. It is liberty you want, not party."[46]

New York School Suffrage Intrigue

The wrangling over the endorsements, or lack of same, made a long summer worse and was further jarred by a new issue, confusion over the new school suffrage law in New York State. It began to look like one step forward and two steps back as politicians purposefully worked to undermine the new law. The *NCBB* was not *per se* a Syracuse newspaper in the way that the *Ballot Box* was a Toledo paper. However, it was very much identified with New York State as nearly all the issues reported the work of the New York State Woman Suffrage Association. Gage had been one of the founders of the state association and five times its president. Another long-time president, Lillie Devereux Blake wrote frequent letters and columns for the *NCBB* so it's no surprise to find it heavily slanted toward New York State suffrage news. Tangled into the confusion over the school suffrage law was the state campaign to unseat the incumbent governor of New York, Lucius Robinson. In an open letter Gage published a protest designed to be extensively circulated across the state. Gage, Devereux, and Clemence S. Lozier, President of the New York City Woman Suffrage Association, "earnestly PROTEST the re-election of Lucius Robinson." Robinson has vetoed the School Suffrage Bill which would have allowed women the right to sit on school boards. And although school suffrage was never a primary goal of the National or its auxiliaries, every step in the direction of expanding women's power and influence was seen as progress. The facsimile of the printed circular published in October expanded the demand to not only unseat Robinson but to include support for school suffrage. The Poughkeepsie NYSWSA resolutions summarized the NYSWSA position:

. . . the policy which withholds school offices from women is not only dangerous and immoral class legislation, but defrauds the children and state of one-half of its best intelligence, morality and wisdom.

. . . that the veto of the woman's school bill by Governor Robinson is proof . . . of the utter disregard of their rights ever shown as unrepresented class and . . . the danger of ignorant power in the hands of a single man.

November brought claims of their success. "Thousands and tens of thousands of Woman's Protests were circulated, sent to every newspaper in the state . . . distributed at political meetings . . . handed to passengers over the ferries most traversed, placed in manufactories and workshops where many hands were employed . . . the work was unceasing.[47] The new governor, Ezra Cornell, had promised to sign a woman's school bill and a woman's presidential suffrage bill that would allow women to vote for electors for president and vice-president and on February 5, 1881, Cornell kept his promise and signed the bill into law allowing women to vote for and hold school offices.

Gage cautioned against mistaking these small victories for the real prize but it must have been critically important to report progress of any kind in the face of so much regular disappointment. The forces against them rallied again by August. A small article in the *NCBB* that month reports that there appeared to be some misunderstanding as to whether or not the new school suffrage law actually entitled women to vote on school questions. "Yes. Women in New York have the right to vote upon school questions on precisely the same grounds as men." To make sure there was no further confusion the NYSWA would be making an active canvass of the state prior to school elections on the first Tuesday in October. But, as the election drew near the State Superintendent of Schools Robert Gilmour circulated a flyer ". . . defining the law in a way to restrict the great proportion of women from taking part in the coming school elections." Too many women were unaware the law had been passed or were intimidated by threats of penalties for illegal voting making it easy to take advantage of them. To make matters even more frustrating, the state's general circulation newspapers were silent on the matter.

In Fayetteville there was no confusion. Employing strategies anticipating Carrie Chapman Catt's strategies in the New York Suffrage campaign forty years later, Gage and her friends rallied the troops and elected Gage's daughter, Helen Leslie, School Clerk; Fanny Ecker as Librarian, and Frances Carr as Trustee. And, they did it by an overwhelming majority of 126 votes. For weeks prior to the election Gage filled the pages of the local paper, The Fayetteville *Recorder* with informational articles on the new law, who was qualified to vote, and criticism of Gilmour. The last week of the campaign she and Anthony held an informational meeting for women only in the Baptist church to answer any lingering questions. Together she and the women of Fayetteville organized a complete slate of qualified women candidates then they divided the school district into sections and canvassed them all. "Private carriages were volunteered" for the elderly and infirm she wrote and continued, "*One hundred and two* women voted and proved several points:

First, that women, even those who say they do not want to vote will vote as soon as they have the opportunity . . .

Second, the fallacy of the talk that men are more willing women should vote that they are to vote, and that whenever women demand the ballot they will get it.

Third, the fallacy of the objection, 'that women will vote just as their husbands do.' The wife of one of the opposing trustees was actively at work . . . with a carriage bringing in women voters.

"The editor of the *National Citizen and Ballot Box* held her place by the side of the inspectors watching the votes until the polls closed.[48] Through her efforts to make school suffrage happen in her own Fayetteville and publishing the active role of women to make important change a reality she demonstrated that intimidation could be overcome and offered a model for others to follow.

NWSA news, national politics, and New York State politics were all grist for the *NCBB* mill. You just can't overestimate the role of the suffrage press in creating a sense of community among women and bridging barriers of time and distance to unite them. The editorials and the columns of the two Corresponding Editors, Stanton and Anthony, the Washington Letter from Lura McNall, and the New York City letters from Lillie Devereux Blake combined to keep women around the country in the know about politics. It riled them up, gave them reason to hope, and encouraged them to strike their own blows for liberty. Progress! They needed to see progress. The *NCBB* gave them all it could. Successful petition drives, legislation favorable to women from all parts of the country, news from English and French suffragists, Theodore Stanton's letters from the International Woman's Congress in Paris, new suffrage societies formed, and reports of successful (and they were all successful) state and local conventions all found a place in the *NCBB*. Where else would this kind of news be found. It was exhilarating just to know there were suffragists in England and France.

The heart and soul, though, were Gage's editorials. The forty-two editorials written between its maiden edition in 1878 and October 1881 clustered around five general themes, with some overlap: citizenship and government; woman and religion; friends of suffrage; personal politics; and suffrage victories and defeats. And, the editorial slant of the paper was not confined to the official editorials. Topical essays such as "All the Rights I Want" and responses to letters, often lengthy, all reflected her editorial philosophy. Only one edition didn't have an editorial from Gage. Her daughter Helen Leslie was getting married, with the attendant hustle and bustle. Instead, wedding greetings from Anthony were printed in the editorial space.

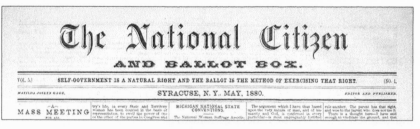

A few brief excerpts from the editorials will give the flavor of her work. As mentioned above, first and foremost on her list of pressing issues was the issue of citizenship. She saw that as it was defined in the Fourteenth Amendment, citizenship was hers. She was a citizen and entitled to all the rights of any other citizen and the equal protection of its laws. But, unlike African American reformers who spent over fifty years attacking *Plessy v Ferguson*, NWSA and other suffragists abandoned a judicial strategy to establish their equal rights. They could have pursued this course. The decision in *Minor v Happersett* was every bit as wrongheaded as that in the *Plessy* decision. Instead, they decided to pursue amending the Constitution. Similar to the Fifteenth Amendment they wanted a suffrage amendment that specifically enshrined in the Constitution their right to vote.

Gage wasn't entirely convinced abandoning the judicial path was the best move. Therefore, she continued to argue for national citizenship and national voting rights. Her editorials reflected this view. No fewer than twelve focused exclusively on this argument. Closely associated with her argument on national citizenship were those devoted to discussing national vs. states' rights. If, as was decided in *Minor*, national citizenship created in the Fourteenth Amendment did not imply national suffrage for all citizens, and its collateral rights to hold office or serve on a jury, then what could account for the four (later six, then nine) classes of federally empowered voters? If states' rights took precedence over federal law with regard to something so basic to citizenship as the right to vote, what rights then did citizenship confer; for what was the Civil War fought? If, as Judge Waite argued in his brief that, "The United States has no voters of its own creation . . ." and any state's right to regulate the suffrage extended to the right to abolish it for one class of citizen, what would prevent it from abolishing it for other classes of citizens, or abolishing it altogether? The answer was swift to come. Two years later Rhode Island legislated an abridgment to the voting rights of over eleven thousand foreign-born citizens. In his Minority Opinion in the Senate Committee on Privileges and Elections, Senator Blair of New Hampshire argued that, "this right [voting] is inherent in the great body of society, existing before the formation of governments. This inborn right, the nation undertook to protect when it adopted a clause of the constitution guaranteeing a republican form of government to the states." No one was happier than Gage to find the Republican *New York Tribune* "jumping the fence" to agree with Blair after agreeing with Waite in the *Minor* case. "It is well for that party [the Republicans] to waken to the fact of its having cut its own throat in that decision. It is a case where a legal subterfuge has returned to plague its inventor." Gage knew a fraud when she saw one.[49] Either strategy was going to be a long haul. The judicial path to overturning *Plessy* took close to sixty years while the fight for woman suffrage, first judicially then by amendment, was a daunting eighty years and more.

Taking Aim at the Church

Religion and religious persecutions and mistreatment of women was a theme that got full venting in the editorial columns. From her first public debate with Rev. Byron Sunderland in the pages of the Syracuse newspapers back 1852, Gage was well-known for her arguments against clerical interpretations of the Bible to deny woman's political rights. The Thirtieth Anniversary Convention in Rochester provided that summer's second heat wave. Three anti-church resolutions written by Gage and passed by the convention caused a storm of apoplexy in both local and national newspapers and pulpits across the country. From these resolutions, the next batch of editorials drew their theme – defending the Rochester Resolutions. The resolutions that caused such a storm simply stated said that woman's first duty was to herself as an individual, a right every individual could claim; that woman had a right to individual conscience in the spirit of the great principle of the Protestant Reformation; and – this was the one that raised the most heat – that the perversion of the religious element in woman by priestcraft and superstition was the reason for her subjugation.[50] Even today, these resolutions would cause heated renunciations in some circles. Gage didn't care a whit about such delicate sensibilities. She often said she was raised to think for herself, so relying on interpretations of others was unthinkable, especially when the interpreting insisted that she [all woman] should be in an immutable state of subjugation to man, church, or state. Therefore, when the imminent publication of the New Revised Bible was announced she was eager to analyze its changes in order to ascertain their impact on women.

What she discovered and reported was that the latest translation was just as bad as any other of the translations. It omitted the account of Jesus's mercy to the woman taken in adultery . . . an incident in Christ's life bearing most mercifully upon woman." To this she declares,

"Oh woman! Be wise; study for yourself, act for yourself, *interpret* for yourself." She and Stanton fulfilled this call fifteen years later with the *Woman's Bible.*[51] Although only six editorials were devoted exclusively to the topic of woman and the church, the on-going antagonism of the clergy toward woman suffragists guaranteed that Gage's hostility toward the earthly divines would percolate throughout the *NCBB*. It was something her readers expected and enjoyed. Her every jab at the positions of the church towards women was designed to empower women and her readers loved it.[52]

NWSA had been forged in the white-hot furnace of abandonment in the battle over the Fifteenth Amendment when women were cast aside when extending suffrage was written into the Constitution without them. The *NCBB* was, therefore, more than cautious when it came to potential allies. Stanton's favorite phrase was to hold them in her "metaphysical tweezers" to see if they were worthy allies or mere opportunists. Most failed its exacting scrutiny. Twelve editorials speak sharp words to would-be suitors. The Grangers took their lumps in the editorial, "The Grangers vs. Women." Responding to a change in their constitution to rescind the provision that all Granger societies must have no less than four women officials, Gage harrumphs that this is just what she expected when the Grangers had first encouraged women to join. They had promised "exact equality" but "some of us who had before been caught by that clap-trap cry, waited and looked on to see what would be the final result." Echoing *Dred Scott v Sanford* she concluded that their action was further evidence that "no woman has any rights men feel bound to respect, nor will she have, until her *political* rights are acknowledged and unquestioned."

Turning to the Labor Party, they, too, were unworthy of woman's support. "Women do not work for it, do not work for any party that does not recognize the exact and equal rights of women with men, industrial and political. Work for your *own* political rights . . ." In "Women vs. The Labor Party" she reported that it had no woman suffrage plank and does not include among its concerns that "woman is paid only one-half, sometimes one-third as much as man for equal work" and works many more hours at home. "The great wrong and injustice commences in the home. If Labor reformers base their demands upon justice; they themselves will initiate labor reform first in their own families."

Impatience with chivalry resulted in a snappy trial for President Hayes in December, 1879, "A Lost Opportunity." A committee of NWSA officers, Gage included, were received by President Hayes "with infinite courtesy and chivalry . . . and all that meaningless attention which giving women, men think they have given them their due – and that was all." For this ". . . we arraign President Hayes before the bar of eternal justice and jury of his countrywomen and pronounce him guilty."[53]

Her strongest criticism was saved for women themselves. "Woman Idolators," took women to task for continuing to support a party that had so completely turned its back on them. Eight editorials were devoted to making the woman suffrage movement move. This group of editorials offered anecdotal evidence that individual women or groups of women could work changes great and small, but work. On July 4, 1879, Gage decorated her home in Fayetteville for the Fourth of July celebration by draping the colors in mourning bunting and posting a sign proclaiming

GOVERNMENTS DERIVE THEIR JUST POWERS
FROM THE CONSENT OF THE GOVERNED.
WOMAN HAS NOT CONSENTED!

To her readers she asked, "How many of you thus protested . . . such opportunity lies in the hands of all." Under her guidance the women of Fayetteville organized and elected a full slate of suffrage women to the local school board, including her daughter. The resulting editorial offered the example of their work as a winning model for political campaigning.

One editorial was a response to an unexpected bequest to the paper. The column instructed subscribers how to support the cause by making a bequest to either the *NCBB* or NWSA, including sample documents. Another offered instruction on how to unseat a governor, defeat a senator, or write and circulate a petition.

In spite of every good effort, however, victories were few and defeats discouragingly regular. All found their way into the editorials. During the years 1878-1881, President Hayes regularly ignored woman's political disabilities in his yearly address to Congress. Governor McClellan of New Jersey vetoed a bill giving married women control of the disposition of their own separate property. The Sixteenth Amendment bill was stalled in committee for forever. Married women were redefined as property of their husbands in the Ohio "Lucy Walker" case. And, perhaps most galling, a bill in Utah was gaining support for disenfranchising women because of widespread prejudice against Mormons. In view of this mountain of discouragement, even small victories were long savored in the editorials.[54]

Most issues had letters from Stanton and Anthony reporting from their speaking tours. Stanton's offered a full range of topics from her thoughts on the church and its treatment of woman and the specious interpretations of the Bible by the clergy to her thoughts on the way the graduation ceremonies at Vassar were conducted when her daughter graduated. According to Stanton, the speeches were good but their delivery was too rigid, the ritual was entirely too long, but she was glad to see women listing their names with dignity, e.g., Elizabeth rather than Lizzie.[55]

Anthony's tended to be more businesslike, reporting where she spoke, audience size, progress with petitions, how many subscriptions she'd gathered, and always included a note to keep subscribing to the *NCBB* and to encourage like-minded women to do the same.[56]

"The Washington Letter" reported progress on the Sixteenth Amendment and friends and foes in Congress. It also chronicled the preparations for Washington conventions and other news from Washington-area suffrage groups. Lillie Devereux Blake's letters appeared on a semi-regular basis as did those from other notables such as Rev. Olympia Brown, Helen Loder, Lucinda Chandler, Sara Spencer and Isabella Beecher Hooker. Add to these, new from Paris, London, Russia, and the Feegee [sic] Islands and sisterhood in the *NCBB* was truly global.

Undoubtedly Gage's efforts in publishing the *NCBB* were appreciated by her colleagues and subscribers. For the first time since the *Revolution* the NWSA had its own newspaper. There is also no doubt that Gage understood the financial challenge it represented. The only support that it could count on came from subscriptions. It also represented a monumental writing commitment at a time when she was also involved in writing the *HWS*. But a newspaper offered a forum from which to educate women to think and act in their own best interests. It offered the chance to circulate NWSA news nationally. It gave women in distant states and territories the opportunity to communicate their experiences, successes, and problems in a sympathetic setting. Obituaries of movement pioneers were occasions for reflection on the work of these women and a chance to share mourning their loss together.

For women who might be the only suffrage advocate in their towns, Gage's identification with the tiny town of Fayetteville, gave them hope that they too could awaken their towns to the great reform of the age, and the courage to try. Gage's personal stamp on the *NCBB*, the monthly column, "Woman, Past and Present," her interest in science, and her expertise in woman's education, acquainted woman across the country with a broad range of scholarly topics far removed from the fashions and housekeeping columns of the popular presses and magazines. Gage took these topics seriously and so should they.

The *NCBB* also provided NWSA leaders with a chance to rebut their critics, frequently the editors of the *Woman's Journal* published by the rival suffrage association, the AWSA. Although numbers of subscribers ranged between two thousand and forty-five hundred, that is only the beginning place for estimating its reach. Papers were often read by more than one person and convention editions often needed a second press run. On several occasions it was used as a lobbying tool and copies were sent to the entire Senate and once to the members of the New York State Legislature. They were also distributed to libraries and college reading rooms. It was a respected newspaper as evidenced by the numbers of publications with which it clubbed and exchanged. There are no clear measures to prove that the *NCBB* increased support for woman suffrage during its lifetime, the increasing numbers of subscribers and renewals suggest that growing support for suffrage can be partially attributed to it. Undoubtedly its greatest influence was with those that were already believers, but even believers need inspiration. The *NCBB* made a monthly effort to provide all the inspiration it could muster and then some.

Saying Goodbye

The last issue of the *NCBB* was published in October, 1881. The announcement to suspend publication was attributed to the demands of completing the *HWS*. This was so, but Gage was also facing financial problems as her husband's health began to deteriorate. This meant an added strain on her energy and time as she began to take over the duties of running the family dry goods store and further explained her decision to give up the paper. She had been concerned about the paper's financial situation for about a year, since Anthony had stopped lecturing and gathering subscriptions. Her last editorial, "The End, Not Yet," was an inspirational homily to continue the work. "To those who fancy we are near the end of the battle, or that the reformer's path is strewn with roses, we say to them, nay, . . . We are battling for the good of those who shall come after us; they, not ourselves, shall enter into the harvest."[57]

NOTES

1. Kohrs Campbell, Karen, *Man Cannot Speak For Her,* vol. I (New York: Greenwood Press, 1989) qtd. in Solomon, Martha, ed., *A Voice of Their Own,* (Tuscaloosa: University of Alabama Press, 1991), 15.

2. Welter, Barbara, "The Cult of True Womanhood; 1820-1860," *American Quarterly,* 18, (1966), 154-71 and Solomon, 16.

3. See "Saratoga Convention, 1855," *History of Woman Suffrage,* I, 624-5, for remarks by Susan B. Anthony on the general press and urgings to circulate tracts and but *The Una* and *The Woman's Advocate* "for reliable information on the woman suffrage movement." And DuBois, Ellen Carol, *Feminism and Suffrage, The Emergence of an Independent Woman's Movement in America 1848-1869,* "The Kansas Campaign of 1867," 79-104.

4. Jerry, E. Claire, "The Role of Newspapers in the Nineteenth-Century Woman's Movement," 17 in Solomon. The essay follows, but not exclusively, the chronology of Volume I of the *History of Woman Suffrage* and quotes Gage's essay "Woman in Newspapers" Chapter 2, Vol. 2, apparently unaware that its author also published a suffrage newspaper for the NWSA. Gage's newspaper *The National Citizen and Ballot Box* is not among the newspapers discussed either in this essay or this collection. As you will see, Gage's paper was actually longer lived than *Revolution*.

5. Stanton, Anthony, and Gage, *History of Woman Suffrage,* 3 vol., 2nd ed., (Rochester, N.Y.: Charles Mann, 1886) I, 625.

6. Masel-Walters, Lynne, "Their Rights and Nothing More: A History of *The Revolution,* 1868-1879" *Journalism Quarterly,* 53 (Summer 1976) 242 and DuBois 60.

7. American Equal Rights Association

8. DuBois, 189-200. Charges of secrecy also surrounded the eleventh-hour NWSA executive session that Anthony chaired in which the merger of the NWSA and AWSA was settled for the membership. (*See chapter 4*)

9. *Ibid.,* Anthony performed a similar public gesture after the merger when she tried to smooth things over with disaffected former co-workers, Gage and Rev. Olympia Brown, by paying for life memberships for each of them in the new National American Woman Suffrage Association. See Harper, *The Life and Work of Susan B. Anthony,* p. 659.

10. *Revolution,* Dec. 2, 1869, 343.

11. *Ibid.,* Jan. 6, 1870, 11

12. *Ibid.,* Jan. 13, 1870, 28

13. Masel-Walters, 249-50

14. *Ibid.,* 251

15. Kohrs Campbell, Masel-Walters, and Dow, Bonnie J., "*The Revolution, 1868-1870: Expanding the Woman Suffrage Agenda,*" in Solomon

16. Between 1852 and 1868 Gage was involved in all sorts of reform organizations: Onondaga County Equal Rights Assoc., American Anti-Slavery Society that became the American Equal Rights Association, Woman's Rights conventions, in fact asking to speak at the first suffrage convention she attended and gaining the attention of Lucretia Mott and Elizabeth Cady Stanton in Syracuse, 1852. She continued as a regular speaker for all the organizations that she was involved with. She joined and stayed in the upper echelons; always "on the platform."

17. *The Revolution,* 1868: April 9, p. 215; April 30, p. 259; May 7, p. 311; May, 21; June, 11, p. 164; August 20, p. 108; Sept. 17, p. 165-6. 1869: Jan. 14, p. 1-3; Feb. 15, p. 119; March 25; July 29, p. 49; & Oct. 21, p. 242-4.

18. *Ibid.,* 1869: July, 22, p. 40; July 29, p. 1; Sept. 30, p. 194; 1870: Jan. 6, p. 4; Jan. 13, p. 20.

19. Stanton, Elizabeth Cady, Anthony, Susan B., and Gage, Matilda Joslyn, eds. *History of Woman Suffrage,* 3 vols., 2nd ed., (Rochester, N. Y.: Charles Mann) 1886.

20. *The Ballot Box,* "Letter from Mrs. Stanton, Tenafly, N. J., July 22, 1876, 4.

21. Matilda Joslyn Gage, Scrapbook, Schlesinger Library, Radcliff College, Women's Studies Manuscript Collections, Series 1, University Publications of America, Bethesda, Maryland. Microfilm

22. *Ibid.*

23. *National Citizen and Ballot Box,* "Mrs. Williams' Farewell," May, 1878, 1.

24. *NCBB,* June, 1878, 1 and SBA to Elizabeth M. Boynton [Harbert], June 12, 1884 and Jan. 3, 1885. Eight years later, on the possibility of "one national woman suffrage newspaper again" and what to name it, Anthony said, "But what would be its name? Why not '*The Ballot Box.*' Under that name I got more subscribers and more cheerfully for Mrs. Williams – wholly unknown as she was – than it was possible for me to do after Mrs. Gage changed it to 'National Citizen.' I could make '*Ballot Box*' jingle audiences? Then there was no mistaking the thing the paper was after. As I used to tell them two boxes women wanted access to – the ballot box and the jury box!! More than half the success of a

special paper is in its <u>name</u>!" I liked the name '*The Ballot Box*' and was always sorry that Mrs. Gage prefixed National Citizen."

Anthony's memory overstates her success for Mrs. Williams and *The Ballot Box* and understates her success for the *NCBB*. Between February and November, 1877, she reported to Isabella Beecher Hooker that she had sent "*The Ballot Box* 350 new subscriptions." She, however, regularly sent the *NCBB* 700-800 subscriptions per year. In this researcher's opinion SBA regularly sniped at and about MJG in a way that she would not dare to ECS. They just didn't see eye to eye although they usually tried to put a good face on it in public. And, as can be seen here, nothing was too petty for SBA to get the snark going. SBA to IBH, Nov. 11, 1877, Stanton-Anthony Papers.

25. SBA to Isabella Beecher Hooker, Nov. 11, 1877, Stanton-Anthony Papers.

26. SBA to George W. Harper, Feb. 24, 1879, Stanton-Anthony Papers. All letters of invitation to the (Rochester) Anniversary Convention sent from May through July included a note to subscribe to the *NCBB*.

27. *NCBB*, February, 1879, 8. Only three clubbed papers made the transition from *The Ballot Box* and needed to be renegotiated by Gage. The three that made the transition were: *The Woman's Journal, Popular Science Monthly*, and *The North American Review*. Williams had clubbed with about thirty "liberal, scientific, and progressive periodicals," seven of which were English or German.

28. MJG to Lucy Stone, Dec. 19,1878 and Dec. 30, 1878, The Blackwell Family Records of the NAWSA, Manuscript Division, Library of Congress, 1975.

29. *Ibid.*, Dec. 9, 1879.

30. *NCBB*, May 2, 1881 and SBA to Rachel Foster, Oct. 30, 1880. Stanton-Anthony Papers.

31. Mott, Frank Luther, *American Journalism: A History of Newspapers in the United States Through 250 Years, 1650 to 1940.* (New York: Macmillan Co., 1941, 201.

32. "Something About Babies," ECS, *Buckeye Cookery and Practical Housekeeping*, 2bd ed, (Marysville, Ohio) 1877.

33. Kephart, John Edgar, *A Voice for Freedom: The Signal of Liberty, 1841-1848*, diss. 1960, University of Michigan, 21. *The Woman's Journal* also had difficulty attracting and holding local advertisers for the same reason, its national circulation. Lucy Stone referred to it as "A big baby which never grew up and always had to be fed." Blackwell, 238-9.

34. *NCBB*, May, 1878, 1

35. *Ibid.*, June, 1878, 3

36. *Ibid.*, June, 1878, 3; August, 1878, 4.

37. MJG to Lucy Stone, Dec. 9, 1878.

38. Several of the state suffrage associations also first published their sections in *The Woman's Tribune* or another of the many local suffrage presses.

39. Approximately the first 250 pages of Vol. III can be traced directly to the *NCBB* or to the writings of Gage and Stanton when they were publishing in the *Ballot Box*. This material covers 1876 to 1883. The rest of Vol. III is given over to state and foreign suffrage histories easily attributable to their various authors.

40. *NCBB*, July 18878, 1-3

41. *HWS*, III, 141.

42. *NCBB*, Feb. 1879, 4

43. *Ibid.*, Feb., 1880, 4

44. *Ibid.*, Feb., 1880, 4

45. *Ibid.*, June, 1880, "National Woman Suffrage Association and Republican Woman Suffrage," 4.

46. *Ibid.*, July, 1880, "Presidential Candidates" and "Woman Idolators," 4.

47. *Ibid.*, Oct., 1880, "School Suffrage in Fayetteville" and November, 1880.

48. *Ibid.*, Nov., 1880, 1. For a thorough discussion of the school suffrage law and women's roles in securing the vote and the results of their efforts see "The Power of Women: Matilda Joslyn Gage and the New York Women's Vote of 1880," forthcoming in *New York History* journal. I did a blind peer review of this article, so the author is unknown to me at this time.

49. DuBois, Ellen Carol, "Outgrowing the Compact of the Fathers: Equal Rights, Woman Suffrage and the United States Constitutions, 1820-1878," *Journal of American History*, 74, 3, Dec., 1987, 861. *NCBB*, "Right of Suffrage National," Oct., 1880, 2.

50. *NCBB*, "Report on the 30th Anniversary Convention," August, 1878, 2 and "Theological Christianity," Sept., 1880, 2. For the resolutions in full, see *HWS*, III, 124-5

51. Gill, Katherine, "Why Women Have no Usable Past," *New York Times Book Review*, May 2, 1993, 13. This is the first contemporary instance where the *Woman's Bible* was credited to Stanton *and* Gage. This was a review of *The Creation of a Feminist Consciousness* by Gerda Lerner. The credit is much more widely acknowledged today.

52. When the suffragists used the term "church" they were talking about the entirety of the Judeo-Christian denominations. The Quakers, Universalists, and Unitarians, etc. were in fact very supportive of woman suffrage. The jabs were directed at those that were not.

53. *NCBB*, "Grangers vs. Woman," July, 1878, 2; "Woman vs. The Labor Party," Oct., 1878, 2; "A Lost Opportunity," Dec., 1879, 2

54. *Ibid.*, July, 1879; Nov., 1879; Nov., 1880. The Lucy Walker suit, involving a claim to property in her husband was dismissed, "as she being property has, of course, no right to sue, for property has no rights against its owner."(!)

55. Nearly every issue contained a letter from Stanton.

56. Anthony's letters were less regular than Stanton's but generally appeared in at least every other issue.

57. *NCBB*, Oct., 1881, 2.

CHAPTER 3

Writing the History of Woman Suffrage and Writing the Historical Record

I brush my hand across my eyes
—this is a dream, I think—and read:
THE HISTORY OF WOMAN SUFFRAGE

> *of a movement*
> *for many years unnoticed*
> *or greatly misrepresented in the public press*
> *its records usually not considered*
> *of sufficient value to be*
> *officially preserved*
>
> —Adrienne Rich[1]

WHAT I discovered while researching the work of Gage was that even the most cursory review of the movement's own documents, including the *History* itself reveals a much broader and more interesting perspective on the movement than a focus on even important leaders like Stanton and Anthony can reveal. The irony is that they toiled, Stanton, Gage and Anthony, on the first three volumes of the *History* for ten years so that the details would *not* be forgotten. So, rather than relying on the misleading and limited credit given to Gage in the Anthony and Harper Preface to Volume IV of the series or the Stanton volumes (discussed below) the evidence to the contrary of their assessment of Gage can, in large part, be found in the first three volumes and in the correspondence of Anthony, Stanton and Gage.

The focus of this chapter then is on the ten years they spent producing the *History of Woman Suffrage*. The nature of the work on the *History* lends itself to a view of these three leaders working together; juggling household and organizational responsibilities, but forcing themselves to continue the work of preserving the past so it would not be lost to the future. It also offers a number of ominous undertones for the future of the movement as well as Stanton and Gage, as it chronicles the ascendancy of Anthony protégées such Rachel Foster Avery and May Wright Sewall and new Anthony ally Frances Willard. These were indeed, years when history was made.

The Centennial, 1876

In July of 1876 the nation gathered, in fact and in spirit, in Philadelphia to pay homage to those "forefathers [who] brought forth upon this continent a new nation conceived in liberty and dedicated to the proposition that all men are created equal." Among those so gathered were the women of the National Woman Suffrage Association. Their purpose was not to celebrate but to protest; to issue a "woman's centennial growl."[2] NWSA was dedicated to the proposition that the time had come to enshrine in the constitution the sentiments of 1848, "that all men and women were created equal." Short of an immediate removal of their political disabilities, they intended to make themselves heard. Preparations for this moment and this national audience began a year and a half earlier in Washington with resolutions to:

Hold a convention in Philadelphia on July 4, 1876, to protest such injustice unless

Congress shall in the meantime secure to women the rights, privileges and immunities of American citizens.

and:

to invite all women in the Old World and the New to cooperate with us in promoting the objects of the convention in 1876. As the enfranchisement of woman would be the most fitting way of celebrating this great event . . . woman suffragists . . . should now make a united effort with Congress . . . to act on this question, that when the old liberty bell rings in the dawn of the new century, we may all be free and equal citizens of a true republic.

To these ends NWSA leaders Matilda Joslyn Gage and Susan B. Anthony organized a campaign to get signatures on a protest to Congress, secured parlors in Philadelphia, issued a flurry of flyers and announcements, spoke to the various liberal associations and petitioned for a place on the program to present their Woman's Declaration of Rights during the official ceremonies. The problems encountered and the events of the Centennial are a familiar story. Suffice it to say they did not get a place on the program, but the Declaration was presented.[3] More lasting in its significance than the protest of the day was the decision of Stanton, Anthony and Gage to begin the work of preparing the history of the suffrage movement they had often discussed. Initially conceived as a volume of several hundred pages, it became three octavo volumes of nearly a thousand pages each. Anthony and Ida Husted Harper later edited a fourth volume, and Harper edited two final volumes with the help of a professional staff of researchers. Although it would be impossible to overestimate these six volumes' usefulness as sources of documents relative to the woman suffrage movement, they have not received more than passing attention as to their production or their contents.

Eleanor Flexner, the earliest of the modern historians to discuss the *HWS*, focused on and perhaps overstated the "grab-bag" quality of the first three volumes, and found their worth in their immense collection of "source material, much of which would otherwise have been lost or remained difficult of access to the later writer." She drew a distinction between these first volumes and those produced by Harper. Acknowledging that the later volumes have a "greater literary smoothness," she noted they were marred by "far less original material reprinted in full, and [were] lacking in objectivity."[4]

Mari Jo and Paul Buhle agreed with Flexner in drawing a distinction between the "intensely idealistic" first three volumes and the last three, noted for their lack of ideology in favor of professional polish. Ellen Carol DuBois concurred dismissing the Harper works as "soporific."[5]

Although all six volumes are valuable, Gage's work was instrumental to the production of the first three volumes only. Therefore, the focus of this work will be limited to those volumes as they concern Gage's contributions. Volume Four is important to this work in that it is one of three sources consistently mined for information on the writing of the first three volumes. Immediately obvious when comparing all discussions of the years spent organizing and publishing the *HWS* is that these discussions are all based on the same three sources, all highly subjective contemporary volumes: Ida Husted Harper's Preface to Volume IV of the *HWS*, Harper and Anthony's *The Life of Susan B. Anthony* and Stanton's *Eighty Years and More.* Unfortunately, all three were written

after the split between the three writers over the merger of NWSA with the American Woman Suffrage Association in 1890, a rift that goes a long way towards explaining why these three volumes minimize Gage's work on the *History* and in the NWSA. Valuable as all three are, they must be approached with caution. Stanton made no pretense of objectivity and Anthony may have been attempting it, but in terms of Gage, did not succeed.

These sources, in fact, offer only the sketchiest outlines of the actual work of all three editors, but of the three, Gage's work as both an editor and suffrage leader was the most significantly diminished. Harper wrote, "Miss Anthony, Mrs. Stanton and Mrs. Gage had long had in view the preparation of a history of the woman's rights movement, which they expected to a pamphlet of several hundred pages, . . ." in Volume I of *The Life.* But when she actually discussed writing the *HWS* in Volume II of *The Life* only Stanton and Anthony appeared. "As Mrs. Stanton's health forbade her going on the lecture platform in the autumn of 1880, and as Miss Anthony . . . dare[d] claim a little leisure from public work, they decided to settle down to the serious business of writing the *History of Woman Suffrage."* As Harper discussed the writing of Volume II of the *HWS*, Gage again disappeared as Harper followed the activities of Anthony and Stanton after the 1882 Washington convention, "The two historians hastened back to their work, which was interrupted only by Miss Anthony's going to the New York State Suffrage Convention." Volume III is again the exclusive work of Anthony and Stanton. According to Harper, "June, 1885, found the two women once more hard at

work . . . Miss Anthony took upon herself all the drudgery possible
. . . and she was compelled to keep Mrs. Stanton keyed up to do a great
portion of the literary work." It is also in Volume II of *The Life* that
the much-reproduced picture of Anthony and Stanton seated at a table
together appears captioned, "Miss Anthony and Mrs. Stanton Writing
the History of Woman Suffrage." In all, Gage's name appeared three
times in connection with the writing of the *HWS* and only then as an
aide to Stanton.[5]

Harper worked the same miracle in the Preface to Volume IV of the
HWS. This has been the most frequently cited version of the collaboration and, therefore, the most damaging. In her usual enthusiastic style
Harper discussed the work of the first three volumes of the *History*: "Miss
Anthony packed in trunks and boxes the accumulation of the years and
shipped them to Mrs. Stanton's home in Tenafly, N. J. where, the two
women went cheerfully to work." Later it was Anthony and Stanton who,
"In June, 1885, . . . set resolutely to work and labored without ceasing
until the next November when the third volume was sent to the publishers." Throughout, the names of Anthony and Stanton are consistently
linked to each other and the writing tasks. Gage was given credit for
only four chapters of the massive three-volume work: three in Volume
I, "Preceding Causes," "Woman in Newspapers," and "Woman Church
and State," and one in Volume II, "Woman's Patriotism in the War."[6]
With no compelling reason to question Harper's credits, historians have
uniformly accepted these four chapters as the
total of Gage's work on the *History* justifying
characterizing Gage's work as minor and she as
a mere "aide."[7]

Stanton's, *Eighty Years and More,* included
Gage at Tenafly the autumn of 1880 but it is the
only place Gage is included as part of a working trio of editors. Further, Stanton's work was
revised by her children and reissued in 1922 as
Volume I on *Elizabeth Cady Stanton as Revealed*

Elizabeth Cady Stanton and Susan B. Anthony at work

in Her Letters, Diary and Reminiscences and eliminated all but two of her original references to Gage, again reinforcing the perception of Gage as a minor player. Gage was not, however, singled out in this revision. Two of her original chapters on Anthony were reduced to one fairly short chapter. Stanton's original Chapter XXIII, "Women and Theology" was eliminated completely from the revision, accounting for several of the lost references to Gage.[8] Therefore, the possibility that the falling out over the merger played any role in these changes seems less likely than it does in the Harper and Anthony volumes. In general, however, all these works have well-recognized biases, and should be viewed with great caution if they are used to assess Gage's contributions.

Gage was no mere "aide" to Stanton and Anthony. The correspondence of the three during the ten years required to complete the work, as well as the *History* itself tells a different story. Analysis of the project that was so important to all three women, however, offers more than just a wider view of Gage's work. It also yields a clearer understanding of the work of all three editors. Further, the story of the ever-expanding project with its disappointments, successes, frustrations, humor, and intrigues is worth telling.

Gage was an established writer long before her work became fairly exclusively devoted to the woman suffrage cause. It was, therefore, natural for her to begin collaborating with Stanton and Anthony on the myriad resolution, addresses, petitions and other documents that regularly issued from NWSA, especially as she moved into the powerful offices of Corresponding Secretary, Chair of the Executive Committee, and President. Gage had, of course, been one of the founders of NWSA and Chair of its first Advisory Committee in 1869. She was soon a regular contributor to the *Revolution*, a sought-after speaker, and an important organizer. There was no question that these three NWSA leaders would collaborate on their history project. In fact, at the time of the Centennial when the work began in earnest, Gage, Anthony and Stanton were also about to embark on another writing project, a NWSA newspaper. Gage purchased the Ohio-based *Ballot Box*, moved it to Fayetteville, renamed it *The National Citizen and Ballot Box* and began printing it as the official organ of the NWSA. Stanton and Anthony graced the masthead as Contributing Editors but the bulk of the project was left to Gage. Anthony, especially, had as early as 1872, come to rely on her as a partner in the work of the association. As Stanton marched more frequently to her own drummer, content with the somewhat ceremonial office of President, Anthony and Gage dominated the "working offices of Chair of the Executive Committee and Corresponding Secretary. These were the offices with the "power to shape and control the society."[9]

Gage and Anthony in Cahoots

In 1872 these NWSA officers committed themselves to supporting the Republican Party and U. S. Grant for the presidency based on the "splinter" on behalf of woman's suffrage they offered. During the summer of 1872 Gage became a frequent visitor to No. 7 Madison as they planned NWSA strategy and issued NWSA documents. A letter from Anthony to Isabella Beecher Hooker written shortly after one of their work sessions reveals a surprised Anthony. She apologizes for not writing sooner [but it was]:

> . . . the dreadful heat and Mrs. Gage's presence from Tuesday last until this morning working out just the right word and work to present from our National Woman Suffrage Association to the women of the country. I like Mrs. Gage and more and more as I see and work with her more-but it seems very odd to get out any paper with anyone save Mrs. Stanton – it is what I never did before as I can remember. But I could not go to her – and there was not time to wait for the mails, so I hope it will please her.

Their address appeared in the morning "*Democrat* and P.M. *Express* with good editorials."[10] This is not to say that Gage usurped Stanton's place either in the NWSA or in Anthony's friendship, but Stanton and Anthony increasingly found themselves on different sides of the fence. Stanton, for example, was much more taken with the possibility of having the Stone-Blackwell forces join them in the campaign for Grant, only to be spurned. Anthony poured out her irritation to her dear friend Martha Wright:

Here is the finale of all the loving, fraternal letters of Lucy and Harry to Mrs. Stanton, thro' the summer – refusal to be present at this first campaign meeting tho' offered their price to do so. I do so hope Mrs. Stanton will not be so fooled with them again – but it is no use hoping, she will be. But for Mrs. Gage & myself taking no stock in puffers, we should have been without any prospect of a campaign.[11]

Anthony held Stanton responsible for the thinly veiled accusations regarding the Beecher-Tilton scandal that appeared in the *Woodhull-Claflin Weekly*. This following closely on the heels of Stanton's defection to Woodhull's People's Convention in May, and her studied indifference to Anthony's trial, made working together tricky, if not impossible at times. And it was no secret that Stanton was not happy with conventions or the work they involved. On this topic Stanton also wrote to Martha Wright in 1873:

I endured untold crucifixion at Washington. I suppose I looked patient and submissive but I could have boxed that Mary Walker's ears with a vengeance . . . two days of speaking and resolving and dreading lest someone should make fools of us all. Rehearsing the same old arguments in the same old way . . . Must this be endured to the end of our slavery?[12]

Therefore, Gage more regularly shouldered the writing tasks for NWSA and Anthony. In 1872-3, when Anthony was brought to trial for voting, it was Gage who helped canvass first Monroe and then Ontario County in her defense and it was Gage who fashioned the thunderbolts Anthony delivered in her speech "Is it a Crime for a U. S. Citizen to Vote?" Although Anthony makes two notations in her diary, January 8 and 9, 1873, that she is "home writing constitutional argument" it is unlikely that she did more than edit. She had just returned to Rochester from Fayetteville where she found Gage's "wonderful file of facts and dates which she [could] produce in right time and place . . ." She completed her first collaborative work with Gage in July, 1872 and then worked closely with her throughout the campaign for Grant. Stanton spent the summer of 1872 at home "heat demoralized." Stanton, who is usually credited with writing Anthony's speeches, was quite indifferent to Anthony's arrest and trial and it is equally unlikely that she interrupted her lyceum work to write this speech when she refused to attend the trial. Therefore, the only possible writer with whom Anthony had previously worked and shared her enthusiasm for testing the law, in fact willing to speak on her behalf during the weeks prior to the trial, was Gage. The speech, which has been lauded as "a persuasive masterpiece, . . . viewed as an example of forensic rhetoric" is also very much in Gage's style. The "complex argument, and the lawyer-like tone" that Gage brought to the 1875 Declaration of Rights is the same complexity and tone found in Anthony's speech.[13]

Getting Started, 1876

While Gage worked with Anthony setting up the NWSA parlors for the Centennial she also served for the fifth time as Chair of the Executive Committee and had been NWSA's President the preceding year. Although there is no definitive moment during the Centennial that can be pointed out as *the* moment the history project was born, Anthony's inquiries for materials and money began almost as soon as she joined Gage in Philadelphia, weeks before Stanton arrived. In a letter to Caroline Ingham dated June 4, 1876, she asked, "Will you, too, give me what you think should be noted of Iowa in our *History*. We want to make it as nearly cover every part and parcel of our movement in every state as possible." June 7, she brings longtime friend and editor of the unofficial NWSA newspaper, Sarah Williams into the project, "And, Mrs. Williams, will you not gather up as many $5 contributions as possible and send on for the *History* as well as smaller or larger contributions to help defray our heavy expenses here."[14] Obviously, Anthony had made her commitment and started work.

Although there is evidence to support the project as the brainchild of all three women, each integral to the launching of the work, the initial announcement of the plan in the [Toledo, Ohio] *Ballot Box* listed only Stanton and Anthony in spite of the fact that Anthony was working with Gage at the time and Stanton's arrival was weeks in the future. It is possible that Gage had not yet committed herself to the project but this seems unlikely as she had often expressed enthusiasm for launching such a project. Or, was it yet another example of Anthony conveniently "forgetting" to credit Gage? What is clear is that Anthony joined Stanton in Tenafly immediately following the Centennial and had her trunks of materials sent there. Anthony was well aware of the copious files in Fayetteville and knew Gage as a self-starter. Therefore, it was just as possible that Gage began her part in the project at home, where she still had an eleven-year old daughter while Anthony delivered the materials and the constant prodding Stanton required. And, Stanton's home offered closer access to New York City publishing houses.[15]

The initial conception of the work as a pamphlet of a few hundred pages "to be finished within the Centennial year" gave way as the summer days flew past. The collections of materials soon assumed mountainous proportions and reality settled in. The first splash of cold water arrived at the beginning of August with Lucy Stone's refusal to have any part in the project on behalf of her "wing." She made it quite clear that she felt the project itself was quite premature:

> In regard to the history of the woman's movement, I do not think it can be written by anyone who is alive today. Your "wing" surely are not competent to write the history of "our wing" nor should we be of yours, even if we thought it best to take the time while the war goes on; rations, recruits and all are to get as we go . . . I do not wish to have a hand in the present one.[16]

No amount of cajoling by Stanton could move Stone to provide "those ladies" with material on the AWSA. However, Stanton's initial request could have been more tactful. Feigning ignorance of their work she explained her need for their help "Being on the wing continuously, Susan and I seldom see the *Journal*, hence are not posted on your work." To Henry Blackwell she wrote, "I am very busy just now collecting material for the history of our movement . . . Could you sell us a complete copy of the *Woman's Journal* . . . that we may know what your wing have done?"[17]

Most of Anthony's time at Tenafly that summer was taken up with her work for *Johnson's Universal Cyclopedia*.[18] And at the end of August they received the sad news of the death of an old friend, Paulina Wright

Davis. Anthony had mixed emotions about attending the funeral, as Davis had wanted repayment of her five hundred dollar investment in the *Revolution*. But Davis had made a particular request that Stanton Speak at her funeral and Anthony decided to go with Stanton, despite the possibility of a chilly reception because, "not one of the old Boston W. S. women will pay the last tribute of respect & I will . . ." She was surprised, however, to find that "Paulina [had] left word for the $500 debt to be cancelled."[19] Much relieved and pleased that Mr. Davis had been so "Cheerfully . . . whole-souled" when he gave her the news, she returned to Tenafly with Stanton ready to work.

Unfortunately, early September proved to be completely unproductive for Stanton and Anthony. Anthony was beset by a persistent cold, her sisters Hannah and Mary were both ill and her thoughts turned more frequently to her sister Gula's death than to working on the history project. To her diary she confided, "this attempt to write our history is simply appalling, it weighs me down. My heart is heavy as if some great sorrow were pressing down upon me – the prospect of getting a history at all satisfactory seems lessening." Instead she and Stanton darned stockings for Stanton's boys "all history work broken." Only three diary entries during September break the spell of depression, ". . . among the papers . . . working hard among papers . . . working among old papers."[20] Critical to the momentum necessary to begin this monumental undertaking was the September 15th meeting between Stanton, Anthony and Gage in New York City. All three were attending a reception in honor of a notable Scottish Suffrage and Temperance leader a Mrs. Parker of Dundee, Scotland. Circumstantial evidence suggests that Gage was wholly committed to the project prior to this date, but this meeting cemented the partnership. Anthony left Tenafly at the end of September with little to nothing accomplished on the history. Gage arrived in Tenafly the second week in October and by the time Anthony returned on November 2, six chapters were nearly ready for delivery to Appleton Publishing on November 9.

November 15, 1876, Stanton, Anthony and Gage signed a contract that would shape their lives and work for the next ten years. In it both the work and the profits were divided:

Elizabeth Cady Stanton and the said Matilda Joslyn Gage shall write, collect, select and arrange the material for said History, and the said Susan B. Anthony shall as her part of the work . . . secure the publication . . . Profits of the History, if there shall be any, shall be equally divided between the said parties, share and share alike.[21]

Anthony left Tenafly on November 18 for a three-week speaking tour of New England. Gage returned to Fayetteville for two weeks before returning to work in Tenafly and do research in the New York City Public Library. Anthony joined her there on December 18 for their appointment with Appleton's. Would their history be accepted for publication by this prestigious firm or not? No luck. "Appleton's couldn't decide" and so they waited for a decision "till after New Years."[22] January 12 brought Anthony the news that Appleton's had rejected their work. "Too hard times for them to undertake so expensive a job,' they said. Anthony was "dreadfully disappointed." Appleton's reeked of the conservative respectability they wanted for their reform and their work. Even Gage had prematurely bragged of this to her readers, "Nothing could be a surer indication of the progress of the woman suffrage reform that the willingness of this conservative firm to take hold of the work."[23]

A Demoralizing Rejection

The rejection from Appleton's rang down the curtain on the project for the better part of four years. A sad little notice from Anthony in the February issue of the *Ballot Box* admitted: "The proposed history of the woman suffrage movement is progressing slowly; the work grows on the hands of its editors ". . . Mrs. Stanton and Gage are steadily at work upon it . . . some friends have already sent us the money and the book shall go to them in due time." This was followed in May's *Ballot Box* by a notice of a letter from Gage to Mrs. Sarah Williams, owner and proprietor:

Mrs. Gage writes us that the work of compiling the full history of the woman's rights movement is so gigantic and the immense amount of material collected on the compilers' hands and to be collected, so great as to necessitate a longer postponement of the final appearance of the work than was at first anticipated. Mrs. Gage is laboriously applying herself to the task, while the labors of Mrs. Stanton and Miss Anthony have been temporarily interrupted by their lecture engagements.[24]

The momentum generated by the month Gage spent working with Stanton that produced six chapters seems to have evaporated quickly when the rejection ended the high hopes of reflected respectability. But other problems also kept the project in abeyance. Anthony suffered the loss of her sister Hannah in May of 1877, and in quick succession the deaths of several other family members and friends. When she finally resumed her suffrage work, it was on the lecture circuit and this continued into the beginning of 1878.

During this time, Stanton did not "put pen to paper" but continued her lyceum speaking engagements, attended the Washington Conventions in 1877 and 1878 and made an appearance before the Senate Committee on Privileges and Elections to plead the cause of woman suffrage.

New Life for the *History*

Gage, continued her NWSA duties, was re-elected President of the New York Woman Suffrage Association and began publishing the new NWSA newspaper, the *National Citizen and Ballot Box*. Taking the lead, Gage purchased the paper from Mrs. Sarah Williams of Ohio and the NWSA had its first official paper since the *Revolution* folded. She renamed it by adding *National Citizen* to reflect the argument current at the time, that the Fourteenth Amendment gave women the right to vote because they were "citizens" of the United States. With the rebirth of Mrs. Williams' newspaper Gage, Stanton and Anthony reunited on a publishing project; Gage editing and publishing; Stanton and Anthony, Corresponding Editors. Although, still not working on the *History*, the *National Citizen and Ballot Box* began chronicling the events and documents that would fill fully one-third and more of the *HWS*'s Volume III.

The first indication in over a year that the *History* had not been abandoned arrived in the September, 1878, issue of the *National Citizen and Ballot Box*. Gage decided to divide the six chapters completed in

1876 into segments, two or three columns long, and publish the chapters as a series. It is not clear whether this was a way to use their earlier work or the start of new work on the project. Anthony spent considerable time with Gage during and after the Thirtieth Anniversary Convention in Rochester, 1878, then left for her speaking engagements in western New York, Ohio and points west. Stanton also attended the Anniversary Convention and left on her lecture tour in September, as scheduled. They had had ample opportunity to discuss publishing the six chapters but no explanation appeared in the *NCBB* until the following February, 1879:

> The especial object of the publication of the Woman Suffrage History by its three editors in a newspaper, is that all dropped facts may be picked up, all mistakes corrected, and everything made right before it is put in permanent book form . . . We have heretofore invited and we still continue to invite the aid of all friends.[25]

The history project was back on the front burner and Gage's decision to begin publishing the newspaper goes a long way towards explaining renewed enthusiasm for completing the work. References to the *History* now appeared sporadically in the correspondence of the three editors, but contained no significant information on the progress of the work. Finally, just when the suspense was about to become unbearable, on August 12, 1879, the silence was broken. A letter from Anthony to Harriet Hanson Robinson details the progress and problems of the work of the previous six months. In it, it becomes clear that Anthony had been working closely with Gage. Anthony had promised Gage she would write to Robinson about her Massachusetts chapter. Robinson had written to Gage around the end of May about the terms under which she would be willing to allow her work on Massachusetts to become part of the *History*. Gage had passed it along to Anthony, who was in charge of the administrative details and Anthony had failed to respond. At the time of Robinson's letter to Anthony it is clear that she is angry that she never received a response from Gage. Anthony explains that she had promised Mrs. Gage six weeks earlier that she would write to Robinson and had failed to do so. Robinson wanted her chapter on Massachusetts's included but wanted to retain full control over her submission. Anthony hastened to explain that they could not take anyone's work without the privilege of revision: "We [can] not accept Massachusetts on the terms you proposed."[26]

The problems reflected in this letter encapsulate the main problems that would be encountered throughout the production of the *History:*

1. The work was done sporadically.

2. It was dependent upon the cooperation of a large number of state suffrage leaders.

3. "Writing" was much more an organizing and revising chore than has been appreciated.

4. Lucy Stone remained adamantly uncooperative, to the detriment of the *HWS*.

Especially problematic to the completion of the project were the myriad compelling obligations of its editors, other than the *History*. Good intentions frequently gave way to more pressing demands upon their time. There were, after all, the three main leaders of their national organization. And, all three felt the pull of family obligations during the ten years of off and on labor that produced the three volumes. All three women depended upon the incomes from their lecturing, thus effectively removing much of the lecture season, September to June, from possible work time. In addition, Gage was committed to the *National Citizen and Ballot Box* from March of 1878 until she was forced to let it go in October of 1881. This extra assignment for Gage has never been figured into the equation and one cannot overestimate the stress of getting out a monthly paper added to the tasks of writing and editing copy for the *History*. These years were also filled with her family's milestone events: Maud off to Cornell, T.C. moving to Dakota Territory to start his own business, two daughters, Helen and Julia, married, and the illness and death of her husband.

Stanton followed the lyceum circuit and in addition, spent a year and a half in Europe where Anthony joined her for nearly a year on her first European tour. All of these events and more intruded on their time.

From the first, the *History* was conceived as a compilation of materials, memories, artifacts and documents. Anthony and Gage both had boxes and files of materials saved from their earliest involvement in the movement, but, if the history was going to include the work done by the state associations, materials would have to come from women in the states. Soliciting and coordinating this material would be the cause of other delays when materials failed to arrive on time, or arrived with strings attached, as Robinson's had. Editing the work of women with confidence and egos to match those of the editors required firmness as well as tact, and caused untold headaches. Anthony shouldered the yeoman portion of this job. Therefore, Anthony, in the position of go-between for Gage and Stanton and the state leaders, usually offered the best source of information on the progress of all their work.

In her apology to Robinson Anthony also mentions "Mrs. Stanton has already written up the early work – down to the war." Statements such as these have led to a general perception that most of the *History*, hundreds of pages, thousands of pages, were written by Stanton. With no intention to minimize the work of any of the editors, or the effort that the final product represents, and recognizing fully that quantifying documents vs. narrative is no way to estimate its value or the work of the editors, it is still possible to show that Gage's portion was equal to Stanton's. That the writing and editing was tiresome goes without saying. Contrary to the published recollections of Stanton and Anthony and statements such as the one above, the record is not so vague as has been assumed nor the work as unevenly divided.

Three points need to be made. First, one of the acknowledged strengths of the first three volumes is their reproduction, *in their entirety,* of the documents produced by the suffrage movement. This has not received the attention it requires when evaluating statements such as this one referring to Volume I, "Stanton wrote all the material except three chapters by Mrs. Gage."[27] Volume I is 878 pages, a sizable portion of which are documents. A look at the lengthy chapter on Ohio completed in 1876, can add some perspective. Of these seventy pages, an estimate of new materials, a two-and-one-half page introduction and the paragraphs linking, identifying, and explaining documents, totals under five pages. The same is true for the larger portion of the chapters in all three volumes. Notable exceptions are the three chapters mentioned above, by Gage, essays on women's history: "Preceding Causes," "Woman in Newspapers," and "Woman, Church and State," and "Mrs. Stanton's Reminiscences." Volume I also contains two other chapters of reminiscences written by early workers, one by Clarina I. Howard Nichols and one by Mrs. Collins. Of the remaining chapters in the first volume, there are ample references to Stanton and Gage working together to support the assertion that no single editor compiled, revised, organized or wrote the rest of the descriptive narratives. No one escaped these chores.

Second, producing these volumes required more than just the tasks mentioned above. They also needed, "planning for volumes, chapters, footnotes, margins, appendices, paper and type; of engravings, title, preface and introduction!"[28]

Third, the role of a brigade of writers has been minimized, especially with regard to Volume III, but true of all the volumes. As the letter to Robinson also illustrates, the editors were looking for documents, speeches, corrections and facts. But they were also looking for women from each state to "write up" their state's history. Volume III alone includes the work of twenty-six easily identifiable writers, exclusive of Gage and Stanton. Further, the first four chapters are in large part materials by Gage that first appeared in either the *Ballot Box* or the *National Citizen and Ballot Box,* as is much of the chapter on New York compiled by Gage and New York leader, Lillie Devereux Blake.[29]

Another problem with the *History* is its "National" slant. This was, of course, unavoidable. First Stanton, then Gage and finally Robinson tried to elicit something, anything, from the Boston leaders. However, Stone and Blackwell held firm to their decision to avoid even the appearance of cooperation. Anthony explained to Robinson,

> When Mrs. Stanton was engaged to write a brief sketch of the W. R. movement for 'Eminent Women of the Age,' Lucy Stone refused to give her even [the] date of her birth; replying to her request with an entire *forbiddal* (sic) of her speaking her name in her article . . . and but for Appleton's Cyclopedia and the broad, catholic & sensible & just sister-in-law, Antoinette Brown Blackwell, Mrs. S[tanton] would have been unable to get enough to make a paragraph. And yet,

notwithstanding Lucy's narrow *pig headedness,* see how generously and more than just Mrs. Stanton wrote up Lucy & B[lackwell] in that book. Lucy, like the South is incapable of understanding *magnanimous overtures.*[30]

"But," as Anthony concluded after two pages exercising Lucy's faults, "enough of Lucy."

This letter gives one final piece of evidence that, though interruptions would occur, the project was moving ahead once more. "We are now going to begin getting our History into book form," and the sheer mass of materials had forced them to conclude, "[we] shall make two volumes . . ." Although they had only just restarted their project, they had confronted all of the major stumbling blocks that would be repeated throughout the work.

On the Road Again

The autumn months of 1879 called Anthony and Stanton back to the lecture circuit. Gage turned to New York State politics and campaigned against Governor Lucius Robinson because of his veto of the school suffrage bill. News from the anti-Robinson campaign front began to percolate through the *National Citizen* along with the news that for the first time since the end of 1876, the summer had produced respectable progress on the *History.* And a letter from Stanton written in November alerted readers that *History* work would coincide with lecturing.

While on the lyceum circuit, Stanton had shared the platform at the Rhode Island Woman Suffrage Convention with Julia Ward Howe and Thomas Wentworth Higginson. In her letter to Elizabeth Buffum Chace, President of the Rhode Island Association, she explained the history project, the editors' philosophy and asked for her help. "My idea," she began, "is to have some capable person in each state write a chapter on what has been done there." The guiding philosophy of the editors also articulated here was to have each state chapter written "in as briefly a manner as possible . . . keeping all personal antagonisms in abeyance. We do not desire to give the world unimportant bickerings . . . but to make a fair history of all that has been well done, and throw a veil of charity over the remainder." Hoping that Chace could use her influence with Howe and thus manage a toehold on AWSA cooperation, Stanton launched a trial balloon: "If the American Association would cooperate with us in writing a great *History*, we will agree that Mrs. Gage and myself on one side, and you and Mrs. Howe on the other, shall decide on all that shall go into the published volumes." She was only partially successful. Mrs. Chace did write the chapter on Rhode Island, but the conference committee was as soundly rejected as every other offer had been.[31]

Final work on Volume I and the ground work for Volumes II and III began in October, 1880. Anthony and Stanton took time away from lecturing to give six months of intense effort to the *History*. Gage commuted between Fayetteville and Tenafly in order to give attention to both the *History* and the *NCBB*.[32] Although the editors were unaware of it at the time, all of the state write-ups solicited between 1876 and 1880, originally intended for their single volume, then slated for Volume II, would become, instead, the bulk of Volume III. Therefore, the months between October, 1880 and the publication of Volume I in May, 1881, were intensely important to the organization of all three volumes, and made it possible to produce the second and third volumes fairly efficiently.

Before leaving Rochester for Tenafly, Anthony fulfilled a few last speaking engagements in Baldwinsville, Oneida, and Naples. But her first stop was in Fayetteville.[33] The newly elected Governor of New York, Ezra Cornell, had just signed the school suffrage bill into law. Gage was determined that confusion over its provisions generated by the New York State School Superintendent would not prevent Fayetteville women from electing a full slate of female trustees to the school board, including her daughter, Helen. Anthony was there to lend her support at a lecture for women only, gather up Gage's *History* materials and "speak" her way south to Tenafly.

Coaxing and Cajoling the State Writers

Once in Tenafly, the letters from Anthony to state workers left New Jersey with steady regularity. To Mrs. Robinson Anthony again had to scold, "Mrs.

Gage said you required us to put in whatever you sent, if at all, exactly as you sent it – It may be we should not wish to change a word of it – But we could not promise to put it in as you say until we see it." To Mrs. Bloomer, "Two things we want of you – a brief chapter of personal reminiscences of your own early days and early work and then we want you to write out the Iowa chapter." A little flattery never hurts: ". . . Mrs. Stanton says Rachel Foster must write the Pennsylvania chapter, over her own name and just as splendid as she can." "Phoebe [Cousens will] write up Missouri . . ." Even Stanton stepped in to smooth Amelia Bloomer's feathers. She had agreed to do Iowa but was unprepared for the deluge of material she would receive. "So as not to offend the dear women that send you such voluminous trash," Stanton wrote, "try and use a little of what they send . . ."[34]

The list of states and writers grew: Elizabeth Boyton Harbert would do Illinois and help with Indiana; Mrs. Bloomer agreed to write up Iowa and her temperance work in Seneca Falls; Isabella Beecher Hooker said yes to Connecticut; and Rosamund Dale agreed to assist Harbert on Indiana. Robinson, however, remained stubborn about Massachusetts. "You do not seem to understand," Anthony wrote once more, "I wish we could have such as you have . . . but if you do not feel willing to let us see and read yours . . . why we shall have to go to press with what we have." Finally asking, "How much would you charge us for every fact you have–that we have not?"[35] They continued to negotiate the matter through Volume II and right up to the last minute on Volume III.

The work continued through October with Anthony and Stanton working in Tenafly and Gage in Fayetteville until she could join them in November. "Mrs. Gage is to come here the 10th in time to celebrate Mrs. Stanton's sixty-fifth birthday, and then we will give final corrections and additions to all we have written down to the war – which are besides what has been in the *National Citizen,* – preliminaries & Ohio, the preface and Introduction, the argument and the chapters on New York and Massachusetts, Pennsylvania and Indiana . . ." Anthony wrote to Robinson. Gage arrived later than expected, on November 19, after getting out the November *NCBB* but brought "some elegant early history of Massachusetts." Clarina Nichols contacted Anthony to describe revisions on her reminiscences that she was working out with Gage and said she needed an extra copy of the August *NCBB* in which they had appeared. Gage remained in Tenafly until December 19, "scratching away or digging into old books, papers, letter for facts." New York State was the center of early woman suffrage activity and, therefore, the most comprehensive chapter. "We are working on New York with might and main . . . we find it hard to decide what *not* to put in – so much of what was said is so good . . . New York is the biggest job altogether . . . Mrs. Stanton spent most of last week writing up our temperance past – Mrs. Gage, the Syracuse Woman's Rights Convention of '52 and the Tabernacle Woman's Rights Convention of '53." Mrs. Bloomer wanted to know what had happened to the material she had written on temperance. Stanton, who seemed to be best able to mollify her, advised her that, "Miss Anthony and Mrs. Gage thought the New York work should come further in the New York chapter with the rest of the temperance work and on reflection I thought so too."[36]

When Will it be Done?

In the meantime, people wanted to know when they would finish. Anthony responded patiently to all inquiries,

> We have several chapters in type already and are pushing the writing as well as the publisher – Mrs. Gage has been here two weeks and is going to stay two more . . . We are working . . . Mrs. Gage will be here 8-10 days more . . . The first eight chapters are in the hands of the printers . . . we hope to see the book done in January . . . it has been a month of hard work for the whole trio.[37]

The promise of Christmas, then New Year's publication dates came and went as the work extended into February, March, and then April. By February Anthony's enthusiasm for the project had soured and her temper become short. Her letters were terse and cranky as she longed to get back to her lecture work. "I'd rather go & say & do & *make* history." As for the other two, "Mrs. Stanton and Mrs. Gage seem perfectly happy in digging away at it."[38] In spite of her hard work on the *History* Anthony sniped to Rachel Foster, "Mrs. Gage hasn't been able to get any of the Convention letters in the February *National Citizen.*" And she resented the time Gage spent on her "church diggings . . . She has given the last two months to [them]." This was an exaggeration, as Gage had gone home for Christmas, published the January and February issues of the *NCBB* and attended the Washington Convention during the two months in question. Stanton and Anthony also attended the Washington convention and for Anthony the break in the history work it represented made returning to its tedium even more oppressive. "No!" she wrote to Olympia Brown, "we shall have but one Church and Woman and this is to be by Rev. Olympia Brown." There is no record of how this conflict was resolved but Gage's "church diggings," *Woman, Church and State*, Chapter XV of Volume I stands as mute testament to who won.

Gage returned to Tenafly at the end of February, 1881 and worked there until the beginning of April completing all the minute details and "pushing the last chapters to get to press with it by May first." Imagine the air of triumph on March 21, 1881, Stanton, Gage and Anthony sent "one dollar to pay for copyright of a history of Woman Suffrage given in the name of Elizabeth Cady Stanton, Matilda Joslyn Gage and Susan B. Anthony."39

With the end in sight, spirits lifted and thoughts turned to the May convention scheduled for Boston. "At the Hub!! Oh, audacity sublime", crowed Anthony when her suggestion to hold their convention in the heart of American territory won the approval of the convention the preceding year.40 Since that time an informal "subcommittee . . . Stanton, Gage, Foster and Anthony of the Executive Committee" had decided to expand the convention to include a speaking tour of New England. And "after an exhaustive consideration [decided] . . . no special invitation [would go] to the Lucy Stone clique to attend."41 The euphoria was short-lived for Anthony. On June 20, 1881, she notified Rachel Foster, "Mrs. Stanton is in full tide for work . . . broke ground on our 2nd volume yesterday so I am not going home just yet, as I had intended but stop and get her started into the work fairly."42 Anthony knew, to paraphrase Shakespeare, Stanton and tide wait for no man!

May's Boston convention and New England tour offered a needed break between Volumes I and II and a chance to digest the reviews of

Volume I. Some "male reviewers" felt a history of woman suffrage was premature while others proclaimed that the movement was dead, most of its leaders dead, and that the rest would soon be also. The *Woman's Journal* felt that the editors had not been "just" to "some women," to which Anthony sarcastically responded when she, ". . . found Lucy Stone's able and impartial notice of the *History of Woman Suffrage*. Well, if she can afford to advertise her own littleness of soul and pettiness of brain, We can afford to let her do so." Stanton was glad to have the first volume out and predicted that "Volume 2 will not be as much trouble as the first."[43]

Volume II Begins

As work began on Volume II, they had not yet decided to put the state and foreign chapters into a third volume. Therefore, correspondence with state writers retained its urgency as they pressed toward a December publishing deadline. At the end of June, Anthony could report that Stanton had started work on her section of "Woman's Work in the War;" and anticipated that Clara Barton would agree to send her contribution on woman's work during the war "in hospitals, on the battlefield & sanitary commission." Already in and ready for revisions were Amelia Jenks Blookmer's chapter on Iowa, Abigail Scott Duniway's chapters on Oregon and Washington; Mrs. Laura de Force Gordon's California, Mrs. Brooks and Colby's Nebraska and Mrs. Harbert's Illinois. Still to come were Massachusetts (or New England), New York, Pennsylvania, Ohio, and Kansas, as well as the Congressional work. Gage returned to Fayetteville and the *National Citizen* at the close of the New England tour while Anthony returned to Tenafly for this preliminary start on Volume II before spending July in Rochester.

Work now slowed to an appropriately summer pace. Letters decided details: pictures for the new volume, chapters to be sent back for revisions, and thank you's to acknowledge favorable reviews of Volume I. Anthony planned to return to work in Tenafly in August only to find Stanton too ill with malaria to work. *History* work was postponed while she made a slow recovery, beset by a relapse in October. Notice of Mrs. Stanton's illness appeared in the August *NCBB* along with Anthony's

September lecture dates. Gage was, for the time being, working at home on the *NCBB* and collecting materials for the *History,* "until the three editors of the *History* find themselves able to sit down together to the work of its completion."[44]

Anthony lectured through September and October, arriving in Tenafly in early November flushed with enthusiasm over her meeting in Washington the last of October with "charming and earnest" Frances Willard at the Washington Temperance convention and the "hosts of temperance women joining in our cry for the ballot."[45] Correspondence during November and December dealt in large part with revisions on the state chapters and misunderstandings over these revisions. State materials were nearing finished form and they had to admit "they already [had] more material than can be crowded into another volume" and they still had not come to a decision on whether or not to try to include a chapter on the American "wing."

An alternative to writing their own chapter on the American presented itself in the form of Harriet Robinson's newly-published book on Massachusetts suffrage societies. Robinson was one of a handful of New England women affiliated with the National. Her book, however, included a chapter on the American. Thus, Stanton decided the *History* could justify "confining [itself] to the work of the National." If anyone wanted information on the American they could use Robinson's book or the *Woman's Journal.* Stanton still encouraged Robinson, if she wished, to submit "a New England chapter."

Robinson's book, however, gave Anthony a "better" idea. "The American is really a Massachusetts society that you could do up in your Massachusetts chapter, then we don't have to touch it at all." Robinson remained unconvinced she could submit a chapter subject to their revisions and worried to Stanton that Anthony was upset with her. Stanton explained that "She's [Anthony's] been unusually depressed all summer with the heat and apprehensions in regard to my illness lest I should be translated before the second volume was finished." But as to the Massachusetts chapter, she cajoled,

Susan, Mrs. Gage and I have always wanted you to write it, that on some native of the state might rest the responsibility of doing the Hub justice . . . It might be well to treat the American Association as you do in your book and not handle the dear thing too roughly. About Lucy's picture, she has expressed herself again and again most decidedly that she did not wish to appear in the *History*. She thinks it a desecration of her immaculate being to be even mentioned by such profane lips as ours. Hence, we have decided to say of her what History demands and no more.[46]

Thus, the project begun in June limped into December and competed for attention with the upcoming Washington convention and the special Philadelphia Convention to follow. A note from Anthony to Robinson in December advised her that Gage was still working at home, "she can work better in her own den with her [illegible]" Stanton, however, now began using the history work to excuse herself from the conventions. A note from Julia Gage advised that "her mother [was] quite ill." For Stanton it meant "That will give me more to do unless she soon recovers."[47] Illnesses and excuses, however, did not prevent the trio from attending both conventions together and witnessing the changing of the NWSA guard. Stanton, Anthony and Gage had assumed the semi-ceremonial offices of President, and newly-created, Vice-Presidents at Large, respectively, at the Boston convention the previous May. The Washington and Philadelphia conventions were the first, therefore, organized and arranged by the new "working" officers Rachel Foster, Corresponding Secretary and May Wright Sewall, Chair of the Executive Committee; both rising stars in National circles and, more importantly and ominously for Stanton and Gage, protégées of Anthony.

Gage arrived in Tenafly shortly after New Year's and the three began work immediately, stopping only to attend the conventions. As Stanton had predicted, work on Volume II was "not as much trouble" as the first. Materials sorted, solicited, and organized during the work sessions on Volume I now slipped fairly easily into place for Volume II. With the trio working together again, the correspondence reflected the familiar cadence of the earlier sessions, "Mrs. Stanton, Mrs. Gage and myself are hard at work on our 2nd volume . . . Hope to get it out by May."[48]

Two Important Decisions

January and February were given over to history work. In March two decisions were made. Harriot Stanton arrived from England and insisted that a chapter on the American, that she would write, be included in Volume II. They also "decided to make a third volume, putting the states, England and European chapters in it. Anthony couldn't be more pleased as she reported, Chapter I of Volume II, Gage's "Women in the Civil War" was completed and "cover[ed] 100 pages . . . and our National battle on Constitutional ground has been a grand one & makes a <u>thrilling</u> history. Gage also finished her chapters "Trials and Decisions" and "The Centennial Year–1876." This last, originally intended for Volume II became instead Chapter 1 of Volume III. As the movement's acknowledged historian, it is not surprising to find Gage's essays selected to lead of each of the three volumes.

With the states also settled into the future Volume III, the editors could concentrate on the finishing details of Volume II. Stanton was eager to be done with it so she could join her daughter upon her return to England and began making plans to sail in May. If there was going to be a chapter on the American, Anthony gleefully hatched a nefarious plot to secure photographs to enhance it. There is no evidence that Stanton and Gage participated in this plot. For this project she dispatched Harriet Robinson. "*Sub-rosa,* tell it not to a living soul, I want photographs of Lucy Stone, Livermore & Mrs. Howe . . . for the life of you don't let a living soul know it is *us* who want the photos!" Anthony hooted with delight at the results of her skullduggery. "I now have two photos of Mrs. Livermore – one with <u>dyed</u> black hair – as she wore it in 1869–70 and the other with gray hair and a cap over the top bald spot – neither is right good, but I sent them over to the engraver." To Anthony's great delight, "Saints Lucy, Livermore (with the cap) and Howe!!!" were thus immortalized, and completed the second volume.[49]

As the format for Volume III was finalized prior to Stanton's trip to England, and its opening chapter by Gage well under way, all three editors looked forward to a more leisurely pace and much less trying experience than the first two volumes had required. Stanton left in May of 1882. Anthony planned to meet her in England in early February. In the meantime, Anthony would continue collecting work from the states. Anthony joined Stanton in England in February, 1883 and together they toured the continent for nine months, returning in November. During their absence, Gage continued work on the opening essay on the Centennial and the chapter on New York State and worked with New York City suffrage leader, Lillie Devereux Blake on the City's segment. Final proofing could wait until all three could work together again.

Plans were made in November to postpone history work until after the holidays. Anthony anticipated enthusiastically in December that if all went well, "we shall get out our 3rd volume in time for the '84 fall trade!"[50] Unfortunately, Stanton and Anthony accomplished nothing of any consequence on the *History* during 1884 and the first eight months of 1885. Stanton was too ill to work from January until March of 1884 and just as she is ready to work, Anthony was forced to take over the Convention report. Word from "Mrs. Sewall [is that] she cannot get out the pamphlet report of our Washington Con. as she had and we all had expected her to do!" Anthony was, therefore, compelled to "take all of the letters, state reports & speeches & all with [her] to Mrs. Stanton's . . . and together . . . first get the report into the printer's hands, . . . attend to mailing a copy to every member, and then begin on Vol. III."[51] More problems than progress occupied May through August. Harriet Robinson's chapter on Massachusetts was still unsettled. It looked certain that there wasn't enough material for a chapter on Kansas, so they would be forced to settle for a "paragraph" about the "state university especially its Greek class and its woman professor," Miss Sarah Brown. Rachel Foster's chapter on Pennsylvania was pronounced unusable. Anthony's new protégées were beginning to look more than a little unreliable. Stanton would have to set aside other work to rewrite Pennsylvania for her. And, perhaps most vexing of all to Anthony, she discovered that an important package of materials on Rochester's Anti-Taxpaying Women's Society mailed to her in Rochester in March of 1882 never arrived and was still missing.[52]

Mid-August brought financial problems. Protracted litigation involved in a bequest from Eliza Jackson Eddy that Anthony had counted on to support the work prevented the dispersal of the funds.

Their publisher was not willing to advance money toward the completion of Volume III. This left them no alternative but to ask their lawyer, Benjamin Butler for an advance of $5,000 toward the settlement and he was unable to do so. No other publisher was willing to take on just the third volume or offer easier terms than their current publisher Fowler and Wells. Without the necessary funds to continue Anthony began to toy with the idea of "take[ing] it in hand myself or in [the] name of the National Woman Suffrage Association Publishing Company." It might be cheaper and had the added appeal of directly profiting the society's treasury and could stimulate sales. But without money, it could be nothing more than an idea.[53]

August ground to a halt all thought of anything further on the *History*. Anthony packed all the completed work into a fireproof safe to await publication the following spring and left for Rushville, New York to launch her fall speaking tour. Stanton, much to Anthony's dismay, decided to stay in Johnstown for another winter. "Johnstown is as good, or bad, as [any] a burial place . . ." but felt Stanton had a duty to live in New York City and be at home to receive friends on certain afternoons & evenings." In Johnstown she, "was lost to the work of pulling down the strongholds of prejudice against woman either publicly or privately!!" Stanton was comfortable in Johnstown, however, and ignored her.[54]

It had not been a productive summer for Anthony or Stanton. The working trio that had been so productive at other times also felt the loss of Gage's presence. While the summer of 1884 ended in frustration for Stanton and Anthony, it ended in grief for Gage. Illness that had plagued her husband since the end of 1881, took its final toll. Henry Gage lingered near death through the summer and died September 16, 1884. Fortunately for the *History*, in spite of the yeoman-like effort necessary to the care of her husband, Gage had continued working on the opening chapters of Volume III. When work began the following summer, Gage was ready with the first third of the volume completed.

The early months of 1885 were given over to conventions and speaking tours. Stanton was also busy with a series of articles written in response to clerical criticism of several resolutions introduced at the Washington Convention by Clara Colby against the "dogmas incorporated in religious creeds derived from Judaism [that were] an insidious poison sapping the vitality of our civilization and blighting woman." Creeping conservatism had resulted in the convention itself tabling them but a storm of clerical protest required a response.[55]

Anthony received the good news in April that the Eddy estate had been settled and she was summoned to Boston to receive her share of the estate, "$24,000 in found numbers." She returned to Rochester May 1 determined to "dig and work for Vol. III to the best of my ability until Mrs. S. commands me to go to her." But, again, good intentions were replaced by work Anthony liked better; conventions and speaking engagements in Ohio and Pennsylvania. Back in Rochester by June, she finally turned her attention to the publishing end of the work. With the money from the Eddy estate she purchased the rights to Volumes I and II from Fowler and Wells and engaged the Charles Mann Printing Company for Volume III and second editions of Volumes I and II. Moving the printing from New York City to Rochester meant a significant change in the working arrangements. Tenafly was close to the New York publishing houses making working there convenient for Stanton and Anthony; less so for Gage. With the publisher in Rochester and Stanton back in Tenafly, Anthony would be forced to commute between the two making a stop in Fayetteville both ways easy to accommodate by train. A new routine was established for the completion of the last volume. Both Stanton and Gage worked at home with Anthony commuting between them and her publisher. By June Gage apologized for her tardy response to letters with the note that, "proof reading has quite filled my time. We are engaged upon the completion of Vol. 3 . . . and all must bend to the completion of the great task, now nine years since its inception." By August Stanton had finished the last of her articles and was also ready to "bend to the task."[56]

Volume III Proves Daunting

The third volume should have been the easiest. Gage had the first sections ready and the rest of the material was being written by state leaders. Only editing, correcting proofs and revisions should have been necessary. Instead, they were inundated with materials that were close to unusable. Anthony complained, ". . . all the chapters have come in the same way, with double the material we can possibly use" and writers reluctant to eliminate so much as a comma from their work." Especially irksome were the endless agonies of Amelia Bloomer and Harriet Robinson over their chapters. Bloomer watched every change like a hawk and was quick to complain. And, Bloomer's constant complaining was exceeded only Harriet Robinson's. Both were guilty of verbosity. Writers were asked to keep their work to under twenty-five pages, both missed the mark. As Gage had written the Massachusetts chapter for Volume I and covered the years up to the Civil War. Robinson was asked to cover the years since the Civil War. Instead, Anthony wanted to know, "why in the world did you open with the Revolution and repeat what we have in Volume I – can it be I never told you to begin your chapter with 1860. When she received no response, Stanton tried her hand at convincing her the chapter "must be thinned – I fear you have never read our history." Her chapter was also a ponderous 55 pages.[57]

Anthony finally blew up at Bloomer, "You mustn't hold me to very strict account . . . I simply do the best I can & know, BUT STILL THE BEST I CAN!!" Stanton chimed in to tell Bloomer, "You are certainly unfair in your last epistle to Susan, in complaining that you have not the full mead of praise you deserve in the History." She continues, using the letter to vent her frustration with the entire project, "I wish you could know what our labor has been and all the carping we have had on all sides. Nobody is pleased with their pictures, with the space accorded them. They seem to think the History written specially to relate every incident of their lives. If you could see the letters we get, the growling . . . you would wonder that we had not thrown up the whole thing in disgust long ago.[58]

By far the most entertaining complaint received came from Marietta M. Bones, Vice-President of NWSA for the Territory of Dakota who had a bone to pick with the editors:

Have received an engraving from Mr. Buttre which purports to be of myself & says he had sent you a copy of the same – would you recognize it as a likeness of me? None of my neighbors do until so informed . . . never was thin in flesh in my life – present weight

170 lbs & certainly there is no resemblance to me in lips or mouth . . . In case there is no remedy and the present eng[raving] must be used . . . I would rather far have none appear in the book.[59]

It is clear that, although in terms of actual time involved on Volume III, it was no more time-consuming that either of the first two volumes. It was, however, the most vexing to produce. In Harper's version the completion of the work coincided neatly with the end of the year, "Her long and persistent labors were rewarded, for the close of 1885 found the whole third volume of the History in the hands of the printers." Concluding the project was rather more ragged than Harper reports. Editing, proofreading, and revising lasted well into the early months of 1886, delaying the Washington Convention until February that year. Finally, on June 3, Anthony wrote to Elizabeth Harbert that she was in Kansas and, "off duty while the indexer and the binder finish Vol. III. The indexing of the three huge volumes is a big job and I hope it will be a good one."[60]

The entire project was a "big job;" one that preserved the "bricks and mortar" of the nineteenth century woman suffrage movement and now stands as testimony to the dedication of the three women determined that our history not be lost. It is ironic that Matilda Joslyn Gage, so instrumental to the preservation of the past, has only recently begun to receive the attention she deserves. What is clear from this research is that sources written after the rift over uniting with the American in 1890 and directly traceable to Anthony and Stanton are not good sources on the contributions made by Gage.

Change is in the Wind

As important as filling in the record on Gage is, it is not the only thing to be gained from a close study of the years spent in this lengthy collaboration. Between 1876 and 1886 it becomes more and more evident that change is in the wind. The "church diggings" of Gage and Stanton that so vexed Anthony will lead both Gage and Stanton to marginalized positions in the suffrage movement by the end of the decade. Resolutions like Gage's Rochester Resolutions that were whole-heartedly passed at the Thirtieth

Anniversary Convention of 1878 will be replaced by hymns and benedictions during the International Council in 1888, once the temperance hosts of Frances Willard join and Anthony begins courting the American to merge the two associations.[61] New protégées, like Rachel Foster and May Wright Sewall, nursed along by Anthony will repudiate Stanton and her *Woman's Bible* signaling the inception of a deadening orthodoxy which will paralyze the movement until the second decade of the twentieth century.

NOTES

1. Adrienne Rich, "Culture and Anarchy," *A Wild Patience Has Taken Me This Far: Poems 1978-1981,* New York: W.W. Norton, 1981, 14.
2. Elizabeth Cady Stanton Susan B. Anthony and Matilda Joslyn Gage, *The History of Woman Suffrage,* 3, (Rochester, NY: Charles Mann Printing Co., 1886), 1-56 and MJG to T. Clarkson Gage, Feb. 8-July 6, 1876 and "Centennial Letters," {Fayetteville} Recorder, 1876.
3. Eleanor Flexner, *Century of Struggle,* rev. ed. (Cambridge: Harvard University Press, 1975) 337.
4. Mari Jo and Paul Buhle, eds. *The Concise History of Woman Suffrage,* (Chicago: University of Illinois Press, 1978) xviii-xxi. Ellen Carol DuBois, "Harriet Stanton Blatch and Feminist History in the 1920s: Daughter to the Past," paper presented for the Seventh Berkshires Conference on Women's History, Wellesley College, June 19, 1987.
5. Ida Husted Harper, *Life and Work of Susan B. Anthony, I and II,* (Indianapolis and Kansas City: Bowen-Merrill Co., 1898).
6. Susan B. Anthony and Ida Husted Harper, *History of Woman Suffrage,* IV (Indianapolis: Hollenbeck Press, 1902), v-vi.
7. *Ibid.,* One paragraph effectively "covers" Gage's work:

   Mrs. Stanton was the matchless writer, Miss Anthony the collector of material, the searcher of statistics, the business manager, the keen critic, the detector of omissions, chronological flaws and discrepancies in statement such as are unavoidable even with the most careful historian. On many occasions they called to their aid for historical facts Mrs. Matilda Joslyn Gage, one of the most logical, scientific and fearless writers of her day.

8. Elizabeth Cady Stanton, *Eighty Years and More, Reminiscences 1815-1897,* reprint, (New York: Schocken Books, 1971) 326-7 and Theodore Stanton and Harriot Stanton Blatch, eds. *Elizabeth Cady Stanton as Revealed in Her Letters, Diary and Reminiscences,* I and II (New York: Harper & Brothers, 1922).
9. SBA to Harriet Jane Hanson Robinson, Jan. 30, 1882.
10. SBA to IBH, July 20, 1872 and Anthony Diary July 16-20, 1872.
11. SBA to Martha Coffin Wright, Sept. 12, 1872
12. ECS to Martha Coffin Wright, March 8, 1873.
13. SBA to Martha Coffin Wright, Jan. 1, 1873, Karlyn Kohrs Campbell, *Man*

Cannot Speak for Her: Key Texts of the Early Feminists, I (New York: Greenwood Press, 1989) 108 and Lois Banner, *Elizabeth Cady Stanton: a Radical for Women's Rights,* (Boston: Little, Brown, 1980) 160-61.

14. SBA to Caroline A. Rice Inghan, June 4, 1876 and Sarah Williams, June 7, 1876.

15. There is a motif throughout the correspondence of SBA's "forgetting" to credit Gage. See MJG to T. Clarkson Gage, June 16, 1876: "I have sent you our address to the Republican Party in pamphlet form. The N. Y. papers give the address BUT COMPLETELY LEAVE OUT MY NAME. Susan Anthony's name is signed to it. She sent a copy of our address to Mrs. Spencer *when I was not here.*" SBA to TCG, April 8, 1903, "I am sorry you were pained at the omission of the mother's name by Mrs. Harper. I think she generally mentions it in connection with the History." SBA to Helen Leslie Gage, "I do not know why it was or how it was that the name of Matilda Joslyn Gage was left out of the circular."

16. Lucy Stone to ECS, August 3, 1876.

17. Lucy Stone to Harriet Robinson, March 4, 1879, SBA & ECS to Lucy Stone, July 30, 1876 and ECS to Henry H. Blackwell, July 31, 1876. Anthony and Stanton were intensely interested in the Boston wing, if only to deride their work. ECS reveals their disdain to Isabella Beecher Hooker, July 5, 1876, "They [Boston] celebrated on the third. Everybody said what a stupid idea, what a stupid meeting."

18. SBA to Caroline Wells Healy Dall, August 5, 1876; William Lloyd Garrison, August 6, 1876; Laura De Force Gordon, August 7, 1876; Charlotte Fowler Wells, August 10, 1876; Clara Barton, August 22, 1876; Matilde F. Geisler Anneke, August 23, 1876 and Marie Zakrzewska to SBA, August 27, 1876.

19. SBA Diary, August 27, 1876.

20. SBA Diary, Sept. 3-14.

21. Partnership Agreement for Preparation and Publication of History of Woman Suffrage, signed: Elizabeth Cady Stanton, Matilda Joslyn Gage and Susan B. Anthony, November 15, 1876.

22. "Letter from Mrs. Gage," [Fayetteville, N. Y.] *Recorder,* November 28, 1876. SBA Diary December 18 and 20, 1877.

23. *Ibid.,* "Letter"

24. *Ballot Box,* February. 1877, 2 and May, 1877, 2.

25. SBA Diary, [summer 1878] and *National Citizen and Ballot Box,* February, 1878, 1.

26. SBA to Harriet Hanson Robinson, August 12, 1879.

27. Griffith, 178.

28. Stanton, *Eighty Years,* 326.

29. SBA to Amelia Jenks Bloomer, Dec. 19, 1880 and SBA to Lillie Devereux Blake, March (?) 1882.

30. ECS to Lucy Stone, July 30, 1876; MJG to Lucy stone, Dec. 9, 1878; SBA to Harriet Robinson, August 12, 1879

31. ECS to Elizabeth Buffum Chace, Nov. 12, 1879.

32. SBA to Harriet Robinson, Oct. 24, 1880 and Clarina I. Nichols to SBA, Nov. 11, 1880.

33. SBA to Rachel Foster, Sept. 24, 1880.
34. SBA to Harriet Robinson, Oct. 24, 1880; Amelia Jenks Bloomer, Oct. 25, 1880; Rachel Foster, Oct. 25, 1880 and ECS to Amelia Jenks Bloomer, Dec. 9, 1880.
35. SBA to Harriet Robinson, Nov. 19 and 26, 1880.
36. ECS to Amelia Jenks Bloomer, Nov. 1880.
37. SBA to Harriet Robinson, Oct. 20, Nov. 19, and 26?, 1880.
38. SBA to Harriet Robinson, Feb. 10, 1881.
39. SBA to Olympia Brown, Feb. 18, 1881; SBA to Rachel Foster, Feb. 13, 1881; SBA to Elizabeth Boynton Harbert, Feb. 27, 1881.
40. SBA to Elizabeth Harber, July 7, 1880.
41. ECS to Frederick Allen Hinckley, March 20, 1881.
42. SBA to Rachel Foster, June 20, 1881.
43. SBA to Harriet Robinson, June 12, 1881 and ECS to Elizabeth Smith Miller, June 5, 1881.
44. MJG to T. Clarkson Gage, Oct. 2, 1881 and *NCBB*, August, 1881.
45. SBA to Clara Barton, Sept. 1, 1881; SBA to Barbara J. Thompson, Nov. 6, 1881.
46. ECS to Harriet Robinson, Oct. 26, 1881.
47. SBA to Harriet Robinson, Dec. 18-19, 1881; ECS to Lillie Devereux Blake, Dec. 20, 1881.
48. SBA to Euphemia Fenno Tudor, Jan. 9, 1882.
49. SBA to Harriet Robinson, March 16, 1882 and April 4, 1882; SBA to Elizabeth Harbert, May 11, 1882.
50. SBA to Elizabeth Harbert, Dec. 9, 11, 1883.
51. SBA to Mary Barr Clay, April 24, 1884.
52. SBA to Harriet Robinson, May 12, 1884; SBA to Kate Stephens, May 13 and 20, 1884; SBA to postmaster, Leadville, Colorado, and Lillie Devereux Blake, August 20, 1884.
53. ECS and SBA to Benjamin Franklin Butler, August 15, 1884. Stanton makes a blatant plea to his vanity and her sense of his obligation to the, "As your name has honorable mention in our book . . . your minority report of 1871 is published in full . . . you have some interest in helping us to complete our undertaking and thus add to your own immortality. ECS to SBA, October 23, 1884.
54. Harper, *The Life*, II, 592-3.
55. Articles written by Stanton during the early months of 1885 include: "Woman's Position in the Church," "The Disabilities and Limitations of Sex," "The Clergy and Woman's Cause," and "Has Christianity Benefited Woman?"
56. MJG to Sophie Jewel Gage, June 28, 1885.
57. SBA to Amelia Jenks Bloomer, July 19, 27 and August 1, 1885; ECS to Harriet Robinson, August 6, 1885.
58. ECS to Harriet Robinson, Sept. 30, 1885 and Amelia Jenks Bloomer, Nov. 10, 1885.
59. Marietta M. Bones to SBA, April 5, 1886.
60. Harper, *The Life*, II, 603 and SBA to Elizabeth Harbert, June 3, 1886.
61. *HWS*, III, 124-5:

Resolved, That as the first duty of every individual is self-development, the lessons of self-sacrifice and obedience taught woman by the Christian church have been fatal, not only to her own vital interests, but through her, to those of the race.

Resolved, That the great principle of the Protestant Reformation, the right of individual conscience and judgment heretofore exercised by man alone, should now be claimed by woman; that, in the interpretation of Scripture, she should be guided by her own reason, and not be the authority of the church.

Resolved, That it is through the perversion of the religious element in woman – playing upon her hopes and fears of the future, holding this life with all it high duties in abeyance to that which is to come – that she and the children she has trained have been so completely subjugated by priestcraft and superstition.

CHAPTER 4

What Could Possibly Go Wrong?

THE union of the National Woman Suffrage Association and the American Woman Suffrage Association in 1890 effectively marked the end of the nineteenth-century woman's rights movement and the beginning of the more philosophically arid woman suffrage movement. It was less a merger than a submersion of the National and its agenda into the American and by so doing bringing an end to twenty years of dynamic political analysis and challenge to the *status quo* by National leaders Elizabeth Cady Stanton and Matilda Joslyn Gage, raising in its place the "Christian" nativism of the W.C.T.U., of Frances Willard, and the "virtuous social housekeeping" with which the AWSA was more comfortable. The process involved in, as well as the results of, such an important shift in perspective for the National weaves a number of threads together. It makes explicit both the extent and the limitations of Susan B. Anthony's political power and vision. It also illustrates how the growing conservatism of the last decades of the 19th century came to dominate the suffrage movement itself. Ultimately, the woman's rights visions of Gage and Stanton would be vindicated, but would be forced to remain on hold for another eighty years and more.

They Merged!

They merged? What?! After years of barely acknowledging the existence of the other organization all of a sudden, without any explanation, we hear "they merged." How? Why? Who negotiated it? Which side came out ahead? Why are the years from 1890 to 1910 called the doldrums? Could it have anything to do with the merger, who it benefited, who arranged it, and who carried the day philosophically? Was it a pyrrhic victory for the ages? Well, yes.

This turning point and the marginalization of women like Gage and Stanton who opposed it, deserves some close attention. For such a momentous event it received limited notice in the first histories of the suffrage movement. Anthony's own, *The Life and Work of Susan B. Anthony,* written with Ida Husted Harper, notable practitioner of the "happy ending" school of historical analysis, offered only a paragraph and one of her signature happy endings to explain it.

> This uniting of the two associations was begun in 1887 and finished in 1890, in the most thoroughly official manner, according to the most highly approved parliamentary methods, and the final result was satisfactory to the large majority of the members of both societies, who since that time have worked together in unbroken harmony.[1]

Nothing to See Here

Although acknowledging that "the members of the National were widely divided . . . Letters of protest were received from many states, and several of its members attempted to form new organizations . . ." and that the executive sessions of the NWSA on this issue were "the most stormy in the history of the association . . ." *The Life* concludes that all was smoothed to harmony by May Wright Sewall's "unsurpassed parliamentary knowledge and Anthony's firm cooperation." In their estimation, "It [was] not necessary for the completeness of this work to reproduce in detail the official proceedings, which extended through two years and caused Miss Anthony to write often, 'I shall be glad when this frittering away of time on mere forms is past.'"[2]

Volume Four of the *History of Woman Suffrage,* also written by Harper and Anthony, offers even less. Chapter X's title simply appears as "National-American Convention of 1890" without explanation until the midpoint in the report:

> The convention opened in Metzerott's Music Hall, February 18, 1890, continuing four days. The feature of this occasion which will

distinguish it in history was the formal union of the National and American Associations under the joint name. For the past twenty-one years two distinctive societies had been in existence, both national in scope but differing as to methods. Negotiations had been in progress for several years toward a uniting of the forces and the preliminaries having been satisfactorily arranged by committees from the two bodies, the officers and members of both participated in the national convention of 1890.[3]

Stanton's *Eighty Years and More*, in Stanton's inimitable fashion, simply ignores the whole thing. The union is not mentioned, nor her presidency of the new association she had opposed, nor its noisy repudiation of her *Woman's Bible* shortly thereafter.

The Beginning of the Doldrums, Yet . . .

Contemporary historians agree that this conservative bent that made union possible, if not inevitable, offered little to the suffrage struggle. Buhle and Buhle declared NAWSA's pursuit of respectability "self-defeating." Flexner identified the union as the beginning of the "doldrums" and DuBois noted, "the result was a suffrage organization that could not tolerate serious political dissent and forced it outside."[4]

Recent biographies of Stanton, Lucy Stone, and Anthony give only sufficient notice to the union to justify their subject's behavior in relationship to it. Elisabeth Griffith's, *In Her Own Right*, summarizes Stanton's reaction to Anthony's growing enthusiasm for a "suffrage-first, conservative strategy and religious alliance." It was an "anathema" to her. "She disapproved of Anthony's strategy and tactics but rather than directly challenge Anthony . . . Stanton removed herself from the merger negotiations. Unable to win, she chose not to fight, but she did not surrender." She admits, "Stanton disapproved of the conservative attitudes of most of the participants" but "was willing to accept reunion . . . She did nothing to disrupt the negotiations." As will be discussed below, Stanton did, in fact, surrender and in the process betrayed Gage.[5]

Andrea Moore Kerr's biography of Lucy Stone offers a view of the union from the perspective of the American Woman Suffrage

Association. Although Kerr's biography does not focus on the negotiations, it demonstrates the on-going animosity of Anthony and Stanton toward Stone despite public gestures of conciliation. In this account Stone absorbed all thrusts and continued to support union with the reservation that it be a "loose organization in which 'each should be responsible for its own work . . . and working together as friendly societies, escaping in this way, any indiscretions which the National Branch might run into.'" A major issue in the Kerr account was the presidency of the proposed association. She presents Stone's suggestion that she, Stanton, and Anthony remove themselves from consideration for the office as an agreed upon condition for merging the two societies. No such resolution was agreed upon; in fact, the NWSA Executive Session of 1888 was spent primarily voicing objections to the American's thinly-veiled strategy to remove Stanton from consideration for the office. Anthony's subsequent letter writing campaign on Stanton's behalf is then seen as a "Parthian shot" at Stone. But, Stone knew that Stanton at the helm would be largely symbolic. Her greater fear was that the "egotistical" Anthony would be elected. Stone wrote to her daughter, "[Anthony] so wished to be President herself! To bring her to the top at last would be such a vindication, she cannot bear to forego it." For Stone, the result of the union with Elizabeth Cady Stanton elected President and Susan B. Anthony elected Vice-president was "defeat and humiliation."[6] Anthony accused Gage, and Kathleen Barry reasserted the charge in her biography of Anthony, of being the source of rumors that Anthony wished to have the presidency of the new association. Yet, Stone's letter is the only evidence explicitly making the accusation, and, Anthony did not remove her name from the ballot.

Barry's description of the negotiations for the union is one of the more extensive recent discussions of the topic. Her chapter title, "The Unity of Women – At What Cost?" promises an analysis of the union in terms of its ultimately negative impact on the movement. An analysis of the opposition to the union should certainly be an important part of assessing the machinations within NWSA and the results of union. As leader of the opposition, Gage should figure prominently in any such analysis. However, in spite of the promise of its title, the chapter offers no such analysis; nor does it assess the "cost" of unity. Unfortunately, although Gage is lifted from footnote status in order to be featured prominently in the discussion, her opposition to the union is seen as nothing more important than the result of a long-standing animosity toward Anthony. In this Barry implies there were no substantive reasons to oppose the union; therefore, those who did, including Gage, were simply rebelling against Anthony in her role as "surrogate father;" acting out an unreflective, personal rebellion. Barry is full of admiration for Anthony, and thus says too much on her behalf. Anthony was *not* "the only woman who remained in the forefront of the movement consistently for over forty years." She may have been "one of the few who gave the movement direction," but that direction was not necessarily progress. "Her clarity," she enthuses, "came from her commitment to her people . . . distinguish[ing] her decisions and positions from those who were only involved in a . . . more tangential fashion." Barry then makes much of the fact that Gage was not at the convention of 1889, (thereby implying Gage's irresponsibility) when union was affected and was dropped from the Executive Committee, a position she had held since she helped organize the NWSA in 1869. Barry's analysis appears uninformed by notes taken during the Executive Session of 1889; notes supporting Gage's protest with regard to Anthony's tactics and what was, in effect, a disenfranchisement of the NWSA membership in the Gage papers, the papers of Olympia Brown, and those of other important actors in this dramatic moment. There is no evidence that her research extended any further than Anthony's own letters and diary and the Harper [auto]biography.[7]

Given this positive description of Anthony's leadership and the "spurious" attacks of the opposition, it is indeed startling to find in this same account that there were some real concerns attendant upon the direction chosen for NWSA's future. The uncomfortable response to the Presidential address by Elizabeth Cady Stanton at the first convention of the newly joined association was an apt barometer of how narrow the platform of this new association would be. At the very moment Stanton sounded the alarm that the association protect its platform against exclusion, the organization had already taken its first strides in that direction. This was the cost of unity. "A very high price" for a union, Barry asserts, Anthony understood to be necessary."[8]

It is not too much to allow that others, especially Gage, did not understand unity to be necessary and thought the cost too high. Barry instead, absolves Anthony's monumental short-sightedness with the sweeping understatement that Anthony was "pragmatic and practical [and] not fully attentive to all of the implications of unity – especially the extent to which the movement became connected to regressive trends in society, virtually robbing it of its potential to redefine and reshape the meaning of womanhood, which was the very goal of Anthony's life."[9] These were, of course, the very results Gage had predicted and warned Anthony about. As for NAWSA, Stanton was elected president but returned to Europe shortly thereafter, much to the relief of the membership and Anthony, in effect, assumed the role of president, much to the dismay of Lucy Stone, appearing to "confirm Gage's (unsubstantiated) suspicions, although few others were worried."[10]

One measure of the result of the union can be seen in Maud Wood's description of the Washington Convention of 1909:

> The meeting was held in the basement of a church and attended by an audience of about 100 middle-aged and elderly women. The first speaker presented a state report from Missouri in rhyme.[11]

These brief accounts of the merger have collectively underestimated the importance of the merger. In this they have followed the lead of its primary actor and then chronicler, Susan B. Anthony. They have also worked assiduously on behalf of the various subjects of these biographies in order to show each of them in a good light in spite of their stubborn pursuit of a union that more analytic and insightful minds warned against. This is especially so in the case of Anthony. But, most importantly, they have failed to challenge Anthony's version of the merger. The fact that thirty years after the merger woman suffrage was ratified and written into the Constitution in no way vindicates Anthony's support of the union or the NAWSA's direction immediately following it. New leaders and new strategies can claim that victory.

Taking a Closer Look

A closer look at the years immediately prior to the union, the negotiations with the American and within NWSA, and the results is necessary and calls into question the very nature of Anthony's leadership, per se. Here there is evidence to suggest that by 1889 Anthony, herself, had become a malleable symbol of woman suffrage still ostensibly leading because of her willingness to follow the conservative women so opposed to Stanton and Gage in order to maintain power. Through the prism of the internal politics of the NWSA it also becomes clear that Anthony was an astute judge of the temper of the times whose vaunted commitment to woman suffrage shifted easily to accommodate the "society women" Stanton chided her for pursuing. In short when Anthony's closest admiration and allegiance was to Stanton and Gage, she espoused their politics. When she found a new ally with thousands of potential new recruits in the charismatic and powerful Frances Willard, her politics shifted to accommodate the conservative temperance women Willard could lead into the suffrage ranks. It is important to view Anthony as first and foremost a politician.

A different and more useful account of the events surrounding the union and the roles of Anthony and Gage emerges from Sally Roesch Wagner's, "Introduction" to the 1980 Persephone Press reprint of Gage's *Woman, Church and State.* In a few provocative paragraphs based on Harriet Robinson Shattuck's notes on the machinations to effect union during the eleventh hour executive session that ultimately committed the NWSA to union, Wagner sketches the broad outlines of the deal. Wagner offers evidence that Anthony actively prevented Gage from attending the annual convention in 1889 by withholding the money traditionally extended to officers for travel expenses, that Anthony relied on a voting bloc of "yes" women strategically placed on the executive committee to control the agenda, that the "ring" opposed putting the matter to a vote of the membership, that May Wright Sewall and Anthony asked two long-standing members of the committee to resign because they had openly stated their opposition to the union in order to replace them with women who had openly favored union, and worked to force the decision for union regardless of whether or not a majority of NWSA women supported it.[12] The irony was that although most of the NWSA membership was already on their way home thinking the business of the convention had been completed, two non-members were present. Alice Stone Blackwell and Anna Howard Shaw of the American watched with interest as Anthony argued to disenfranchise the NWSA membership, indeed arguing that a vote by the membership was unnecessary, while at the same time agreeing to allow the AWSA to delay its confirmation of the union until it had conducted a mail-in poll of its members!

As is often the case with organizational ruptures, the 20:20 vision of hindsight clearly predicts their inevitability. Such is the case in the instance of Matilda Joslyn Gage's separation from Anthony's jerry-rigged National American Woman Suffrage Association in 1890. As early as the May, 1881, convention at which Anthony's "nieces" took their places in the working offices of Chair of the Executive Committee and Corresponding Secretary, there were signs of the new organizational order to come. The installation of May Wright Sewall and Rachel Foster [later Rachel Foster Avery], whose lines of loyalty were to Anthony individually, rather than to any set of ideals or to the NWSA had far-reaching implications for both the organization and the movement itself. From that point on the association became increasingly hierarchical, increasingly the lengthened shadow of Anthony, and increasingly ideologically opportunistic, then conservative, and ultimately bankrupt. At the same time Gage and Stanton, as well as other prominent NWSA lights, were effectively marginalized by an association firmly controlled by Anthony and her sycophantic minions. By the time of the actual merger her power would be such that she could manipulate the event confident that there was no countervailing force capable of thwarting her. In this way the path was clear for her sixteen-year reign as the head of the suffrage association; in fact, she became the very embodiment of woman suffrage, a position she retains to this day. Therefore, the events leading to the actual merger of the National with the America, Anthony's strategies to effect the merger and the aftermath offer compelling insights in the organizational and ideological transformation of the movement. Much of this process can be seen in relation to Gage, particularly when turning to testimony other than Anthony's to describe the personalities and events associated with this transformation.

There was no obvious tectonic shift in the NWSA elections of 1881 as new names joined the old on the roster of officers. The only fuss had occurred the preceding year, involving the deposing of Sara Andrews Spencer from the position of Corresponding Secretary. According to Anthony, Spencer was "bright, brainy and executive – but [had] a fearful tongue against each and everyone of her co-workers in turn." Spencer was, however, unwilling to be set aside easily. When the nominating committee attempted to nominate someone else she "pleaded" for the post "thus bulldozed herself into office *none* of the committee feeling it wise to publicize the *real* reasons for their not supporting her." When directed to turn materials over to the Recording secretary, Mrs. Sheldon, she (Spencer) refused and "to this day she has refused to deliver . . . a single letter received either before or since her resignation."13 As a result, in 1881, the position of Corresponding Secretary was open. Anthony, therefore, used the opportunity to nominate one of her personal favorites, Rachel Foster, to the position. At the time there appeared to be nothing untoward in the move.

Time for Change

The general feeling in 1881 expressed among the three leaders, Stanton, Anthony, and Gage, was that the time had come to bring younger women into the working offices. Stanton was content to retain the largely ceremonial office of President, Anthony and Gage were elected Vice-presidents at Large, with Gage retiring from her seat as Chair of the powerful Executive Committee. She explained later, "When I refused the nomination of Chair of the Executive Committee in 1881 at Boston, it was because I felt that younger persons ought to do the hard work that had been mine for years and so I nominated my own successor in Mrs. Sewall of Indianapolis who has filled the place since."14 At the time Gage was 56, Anthony 61, and Stanton 66. Each had devoted thirty and more years to suffrage work and all three were still deeply involved with producing Volume II and soon Volume III of the *History*. Gage was also, at this point, still single-handedly publishing the *National Citizen*. It was reasonable to delegate responsibility. The newcomers to high NWSA offices, however, needed direction and guidance. For this they turned to Anthony who, in this way, actually gained control of three offices. The positions of Corresponding Secretary and Chair of the Executive Committee were not only the "working" offices but the centers of power in NWSA with the "power to shape and control" the association. Sewall and Foster had already demonstrated their devotion to Anthony by initiating celebrations of her birthday and presentations of floral offerings to her during NWSA conventions. For her part, Anthony supported holding the May, 1880 Anniversary Convention in Sewall's Indianapolis and a two-day convention in Foster's Philadelphia immediately following the 1882 Washington Convention. Although there was nothing sinister in any of these demonstrations of affection, for the first time since its inception a mentor-acolyte relationship obtained among the officers. An organization of equals was becoming a hierarchy.

Stanton, always secure in both her position as acknowledged founder of the movement, and in Anthony's overweening need for the imprimatorial effect of her presence at official functions, took a casual approach to the new workers. Her reaction to Anthony's appeals to her "friendship, conscience, everything noble . . . to take the first train to Indianapolis" for the convention and the series of Chicago area conventions to follow, was to tell her son, "I shall remain at home to listen to my own coaxing whippoorwill."[15] Would she attend Washington and Philadelphia to follow? Anthony's enthusiasm was boundless at the thought, "She is equipping herself with a new hat, coat, and silk gloves with this seeming to me of going to the Washington convention and Philadelphia, too, I think she means to go . . ."[16] Therefore, Stanton's own prestige and Anthony's enthusiasm precluded any immediate vulnerability for Stanton. Also, Stanton rarely became involved in the actual preparations for the NWSA conventions. She would, if coaxed into attending, instead, write and deliver speeches, preside at the various sessions, prepare resolutions, attend meetings of the Executive Committee, and testify before Congress on behalf of the suffrage. Her contact, therefore, with the work of the new officers was limited.

Gage and the New Recruit: Darling Rachel

Gage, however, remained closely involved with the NWSA work, especially while she was publishing the NWSA newspaper. And she continued
her close association with Stanton and Anthony throughout the 1880s as
they worked on and completed the last two volumes of the *History*. She
also stayed closely involved with NWSA work and Anthony writing resolutions, and planning, organizing, and speaking at NWSA national and
state conventions. Her relationship with Anthony, however, began to show
small signs of deterioration as Anthony began favoring her new associates.
Problems arose soon after the installation of the new officers. Gage was
unused to dealing with officers who were incapable of holding their own
and, as been noted, she had "an appalling frankness of speech . . . [and]
one was never in doubt as to where [she] stood."[17] This frankness apparently intimidated Anthony's young coterie, especially Rachel Foster. Within
several months of Foster's election as Corresponding Secretary Anthony
felt compelled to soothe her hurt feelings. "From a word Mrs. Gage said
in her letter to me, I fear she has been saying something sort-a-cross to
you – about time of speaking. If she has, never mind it – your young heart
and shoulders must learn to bear the crotchets of all sorts of people, and
not get broken or hurt under them."[18]

Six years later Foster still needed Anthony's soothing. Anthony had
mailed Foster some general criticism about the wordiness of NWSA
women from Stanton written in response to several drafts of the Call for
the International Council, all written by different women. Now Foster
was upset with Stanton's frankness and Anthony again soothed her hurt
feelings with a teasing, "If you take Mrs. Stanton's *thinking aloud* to SBA
so seriously, I shan't send you any more of them.[19]

Foster was an immediate favorite of Anthony's, if we can judge
from letters addressed to "My dear darling Rachel" and "Dear Darling
Rachel," terms she had never used when addressing either Stanton or
Gage or any other suffrage associate to this point. Anthony was, however, overconfident about darling Rachel's abilities and there were some
important limitations to her competence. Anthony promoted this inex-
perienced twenty-two-year old from a prominent Philadelphia family to

a major office in the NWSA. Only months earlier she had asked her to write a chapter for the *History* on Pennsylvania. Then, in an egregious breach of trust, revealed personal financial information about Gage to Foster, without Gage's knowledge, in an attempt to persuade her to take over the *National Citizen* should Gage have to give it up.[20] Such exaggerated confidence and intimate revelations must have given Foster an elevated sense of her own importance, especially *vis à vis* Gage. Her "chapter", however, was unusable, subsequently written by Stanton, and the possibility of her taking over the *National Citizen* quietly abandoned.

It is not difficult to imagine Foster finding Gage's less starry-eyed appraisal of her efforts intimidating. Gage, she complained in a letter to Anthony, made her "nervous." Anthony's response to Foster's nervousness was a willing betrayal of in invaluable co-worker of thirty years. In contrast to her enthusiasm over the mere possibility that Stanton might attend the 1882 Washington-Philadelphia conventions, her attitude toward Gage's presence was a callous indifference:

> You mustn't make me decide whether you ask Mrs. Gage to the Philadelphia Convention . . . I note here again your feelings about Madam Gage. I [illegible] to sympathize with you very much – still you'll be braver and stronger if you nerve up to the endurance of letting the "logic of events" decide the question . . . It will really seem invidious for you not to ask her if she will speak at the Philadelphia – as well as at the Washington Convention – and yet – there is no reason why it should. She wrote us of your ½ pay offer and said . . . that even with it was very doubtful she could go. So there let it rest – for if she makes you nervous she'll do more harm than good – for Philadelphia depends on your being "right side up . . ."[21]

It would be a mistake to give this single exchange more importance that it deserves since all the correspondence among the suffrage women is permeated with private intrigues and garden-variety gossip. Further, two weeks after Anthony's hopes were raised that Stanton would go to the convention; Stanton wrote to Lillie Devereux Blake, "I cannot attend any conventions this season as I shall be compelled to work every day to get Vol. II out in May . . . Susan has been in town looking after business matters. I have no doubt she will go the rounds . . . as she never gets tired of conventions."[22] In spite of the pecking among themselves, a week later Anthony reported to Euphemia Tudor that "Mrs. Stanton, Mrs. Gage and myself are hard at work on our 2nd volume of woman suffrage history . . . we shall stop long enough to go to the Washington convention next week, we are guests of Mrs. Spofford of the Rigg's house."[23] True to this last letter, all three attended the round of conventions, stayed together with Mrs. Spofford and were listed on the invitations and programs as the featured speakers.[24]

Therefore, the letter to Foster about Gage could be interpreted to suggest little more than Foster needing sympathy and support and Anthony's willingness to provide it at her coworker's expense. But, there is a qualitative difference worth noting between Anthony's remarks to Foster and Stanton's planting a snipe about Anthony in Devereux's ear and that is the difference between confidences between friends who have worked together for decades and the undermining of an ally to a newcomer. Again, it is the difference between an association among equals and a hierarchy.

As a result of Anthony's role as mentor of the new officers, she was now in the position of both guiding their work and being influenced by their political perspective. Foster and Sewall representatives of a new generation of suffrage advocates, were more conservative than the old guard and free of the baggage of old animosities. Anthony herself, less in the company of Stanton and Gage once the *History* was complete, continued to look for new recruits for the movement and began to find organizations of conservative women, such as Frances Willard's Women's Christian Temperance Union a tempting source now that they had proclaimed their support for the suffrage. Their reasons for this change in their political stance were less important to Anthony than their advocacy by the late 1880s.

Enter the AWSA and the WCTU

A look at Anthony's thoughts on this organization and the AWSA during the early years of the 1880s offers a measure by which to judge the distance she had traveled by the end of the decade. While Stanton and Gage were Anthony's closest political reference points, she clearly articulated reasons to distance NWSA from organizations like the AWSA and the WCTU. "Our only difference from the American Society," she begins reasonably to Elizabeth Herbert, "is that they place men in official positions and we do not. And it is that little difference that makes our society a live one and theirs a dead one . . . for men cannot make women's disenfranchisement hurt them as it does us."[25] The more important difference between the National and the American was, of course, the difference in their working strategies. Explained Anthony, "We go to Congress instead of the state legislatures . . . that we must among us all make as clear as the noonday sun." a point she wanted Harbert to, 'write and publish' for those who may not be informed on the issue."[26] "Unite with 'her ladyship?'" she scoffed as she referred to Lucy Stone, "others had tried only to get 'snubbed and dropped' by them."[27] In this, Anthony had felt their rebuff when her early attempt to have them join the National for the May, 1870 convention had been ignored. Thereafter, whether it was the role of men, the national vs. state strategy, or Anthony's (and in this she was joined whole-heartedly by Stanton) personal animosity toward Lucy Stone, the two associations remained separate.

Temperance women presented a different problem with regard to affiliation. Most NWSA women, including Anthony, had their activist roots in temperance associations. The women of the WCTU in the early years of the 1880s, however, were conservative Christian women openly opposed to woman suffrage, Susan B. Anthony, and the women associated with her. But Anthony had been favorably impressed with Frances Willard from their first meeting and her WCTU offered a tempting new source of suffrage recruits. "If only we can get them lifted out of their narrowness, they will be a splendid help to general suffrage."[28] After attending the October, 1881, WCTU she was further encouraged. "What an impetus our movement now has in the hosts of temperance women joining in our cry for the ballot!! I am full of new hope."[29]

As allies, however, she was warier. In 1883, NWSA leaders were questioned about their interest in a "conference between the leaders of the temperance and woman suffrage movements." Anthony replied,

"I should be very glad to meet the temperance leaders, but I do not see what could come of it practically. They as temperance women can ask the ballot only as a weapon with which to fight their battle, as a means to an end while we ask it wholly and solely on the ground of right." She also saw ideological problems. Possession of the ballot "shall prove a means to one end or another! Whether it gives us prohibition or license of the liquor traffic! They would need to have their petitions and memorials state that they made the claim for one specific reason with which only a fraction of our woman suffrage women could unite!"[30] Therefore, if WCTU members joined a suffrage organization, they joined the American.

Volume III of the *History* was published in 1886 and marked the end of the intense ten-year relationship between Stanton, Gage, and Anthony. From that point on differences among the three leaders defined the differences in the NWSA itself. Both Stanton and Gage continued to expand their investigations of woman's position in society and the source of her disabilities; what Anthony referred to as their "church diggings." Stanton coordinated reviewers to help with her new project, *The Woman's Bible* and took every opportunity to spend time in Europe with her daughter Harriet. Gage collected material for her new publishing venture, *Woman, Church and State*. Though still active in NWSA as a Vice-president she too took time for her children and grandchildren. Anthony, instead, narrowed her focus to a single-minded pursuit of woman suffrage.

Anthony Takes the Helm

From 1885 on, with Stanton frequently in Europe, Anthony gradually became the person most closely associated with the cause of woman suffrage; *became* woman suffrage in the mind of the public. Now leading and being led by her younger protégés, this new generation of suffrage women, Anthony gradually adopted the mantle of their more conservative perspective. In many ways this perspective was, in fact, a better fit for Anthony than Stanton's and Gage's radicalism. Anthony had never been as interested in their more philosophical concerns and chafed at their interest in what she felt were "side issues." Therefore, it is even more startling to find Anthony actually jettisoning woman suffrage, the one issue to which she gave preeminent importance, in order to cobble together a union between the National and the American associations. By 1889 Anthony had moved from a position of hostility toward the American and Lucy Stone and relative indifference toward the WCTU to the position that union was imperative, no matter what the cost. And the price, indeed, was high.

Anthony's swing to a more conservative agenda did not go unnoticed. It was viewed with alarm by a number of prominent women who turned to Gage to use her power to challenge this direction. So, after seven years in the vice-presidency of the NWSA she agreed to step forward and stand for election to her old office, Chair of the Executive Committee in 1888. Her alarm is palpable as she writes to her son.

As Chair of the Executive Committee for NWSA I need money. Our association has been steered into an orthodox pit-hole by Miss Anthony and her aides and it needs not only a strong will, but money to put us back. You would scarcely believe that even Mrs. Stanton has been dictated to and outrageously treated by Susan and some of her younger aides. She has both told me and written me in regard to it. This spring the pressure upon me to take it [the position] again was very strong and as I recognized the crucial position of the association I allowed my name to stand . . . so I am in the place which requires a strong, steady hand with money at command. The opposition has money and spends it freely. I have brains, will, and the sustaining hand of mercy.[31]

In the five years between 1883, when Anthony expressed her doubts regarding the practicality of even meeting with the temperance women, and 1888, she became fully committed to their incorporation. Her personal admiration for Frances Willard goes a long way toward explaining this amazing reversal. A hallmark of the correspondence between the women of the suffrage movement was its formality of address. In forty years of correspondence Anthony never addressed Stanton as anything other than "Dear Mrs. Stanton or My Dear Mrs. Stanton." How startling then to find Anthony's correspondence with Willard move quickly from the standard "Dear Miss Willard" to the fawning, "My dear precious St. Frances," not unlike the treacly way she addressed her dear Rachel. Anthony's new allegiance to Willard had ominous implications for the NWSA. The first arena in which this became obvious was the International Council of Women in 1888.

The International Council of Women, 1888

The three leaders of the National had very different agendas for the Council. Stanton hoped to have her Bible Convention coincide with the Council. "Immediately after that [the Council] while the foreign ladies are here, we shall have our Bible Convention in New York . . ."[32] Anthony anticipated that the Council, marking as it did, the fortieth anniversary of the Seneca Falls Convention would be the appropriate moment to "leave the helm of the National ship to Rachel, Mrs. Sewall, Shattuck, Colby and others . . . [the time has come] that we older ones must learn to surrender our wills to those who do the work." Of course, now that her protégés held the reins of power, it would be easy for her to talk of stepping aside. She also hoped the Council proceedings would conclude with "the union" of the National and the American. The National had received an overture to unite from the American at the end of October, 1887, and Anthony was more than hopeful that the two associations could unite on the fortieth anniversary of Seneca Falls.[33]

Gage came to assess the dimension to which the orthodox had taken hold of the NWSA and, if necessary, take back the position of Chair of the Executive Committee at the NWSA convention following the Council. And once more she began a close working relationship with Anthony, Foster, and Sewall. Arrangements for the Council needed to be made and Stanton's involvement from England was limited to editing and reworking the Council's Call, Invitation, and other paperwork. Both Gage and Stanton wanted to include sessions based on their church-related research and Gage suggested that "an evening discussion of Biblical questions affecting woman's position before the world, law, church, and family, well advertised would bring tremendous audiences."

She also cautioned Anthony, "Don't give our Sundays to outside people like Miss Willard."[34]

Stanton wrote that she wanted a session "on church and priest causing woman's degradation" which Anthony opposed on the grounds that "it would make it necessary that Willard and church women get their say too . . . I have written Mrs. Stanton," she told Foster, "on all the absurdities of her suggestions."[35]

In order to bring Willard, Stanton, and Gage together in one council, Anthony was determined that Stanton and Gage modify their views against the church lest they offend Willard and her devoted troops, thus alienating potential suffrage allies, allies about which Stanton and Gage had strong reservations, and at times undisguised hostility. Their antipathy toward the WCTU's agenda was rooted not in an antipathy to the temperance cause but rather to the rest of its political agenda. Although the WCTU is well known for its anti-liquor stance, it is less well known for the full spectrum of its political views. Under the aegis of Frances Willard, the WCTU campaigned vigorously to write its brand of Christianity into the United State Constitution. In resolutions passed at the 16th WCTU Convention the association confirmed the contradictory notion that:

> While discountenancing all union of church and state, we do affirm our belief that God in Christ is the King of nations and as such should be acknowledged in our government and His Word made the basis of our laws.[36]

The WCTU also shared members with other associations seeking similar ends, such as the National Reform Association. This group ratified the following in the preamble to its constitution:

> Believing that Almighty God is the source of all power and authority in civil government; that the Lord Jesus Christ is the Ruler of nations; and that the revealed will of God is of supreme authority in civil affairs . . .
>
> Believing that a written constitution ought to contain explicit evidence of the Christian character and purpose of the nations which

frames it, and perceiving the silence on the United States Constitution in this respect is used as an argument against all that is Christian in the usage and administration of our government . . . we pledge ourselves to God and to one another to labor for the ends herein set forth . . . 37

Specific legislation endorsed by these groups included Sunday "blue laws," prayer in public schools, and rigid divorce laws, as well as prohibition. Most WCTU women who supported woman suffrage did so to legislate a particular moral order, and most had also joined the more like-minded American Woman Suffrage Association rather than the National.

Just weeks prior to the International Council, Stanton published a repudiation of the Prohibition Party's resolution to "introduce the name of God into our political platforms, [and] our state and national constitutions." She also cautioned Anthony that "We who understand the dangers threatened in the Prohibition movement . . . must not be dazzled by the promise of a sudden acquisition of numbers to our platform with the widespread influence of the church behind than, if with all this is coming a religious proscription, that will undermine the secular nature of our government."38

Confirming all of Stanton's and Gage's misgivings and warnings the International Council marked an important departure from the types of conventions associated with the National. The effort to please the American and the WCTU exhibited itself in sessions featuring hymn singing, prayers and benedictions. In response, Gage decided to open her Thursday morning session with an invocation sure to set off fireworks. She pressed Isabella Beecher Hooker into service to deliver an invocation calling on the divine MOTHER and father to bestow their blessings. She followed this with a blast at the religious symposium chaired by Anthony. She berated her colleagues, all advocates of progress for women, for the "Almost universal unanimity with which the delegates, both ministerial and lay, in invocation and speech, have ignored the feminine in the divinity."

She continued:

So notable has this non-recognition been, that the morning when I presided over its proceedings I was in some little trouble to find the woman far enough advanced in theology to recognize the divine motherhood . . . All thoughtful persons, and foremost among them should be the women here represented, must be aware of the historical fact that the prevailing religious ideas in regard to woman has been the base of all their restrictions and degradation.

Such pronouncements at National conventions had been standard fare for years, always raising a storm of protest in the general circulation press. This time the storm raged in the council and the suffrage press. Letters both supporting and denouncing Gage continued in the "Letters" column of the *Women's Tribune* from March until August, 1888, when Gage dropped another bomb on their sensibilities and a new spate of fury was unleashed. In a private letter to Stanton, she referred to Willard as the most dangerous person upon the American continent. See below for more on this.[39]

Needless to say, union was not accomplished at the NWSA Convention following the Council. Gage was instead re-elected Chair of the Executive Committee with the hope that she could turn the association away from the direction initiated by the Anthony, Sewall, Foster junta. In executive session the American's proposal was set aside and a counter proposal sent. In this the National proposed that the two associations hold a joint conference to work out the details of uniting followed by a vote to ratify it in each association, one vote for every twenty-five members. As NWSA's membership was far larger than the AWSA's, it was designed to be rejected. This session of the Executive Committee marked the first time that anyone outside of the Anthony coterie had had the opportunity to actually read the AWSA proposal. They were appalled at what it contained. Lucy Stone sent the AWSA proposal to Anthony in late October, 1887, then met with her in early February, 1888, anticipating that the NWSA convention following the International Council would ratify the union.[40] Stone was correct in her assumption that after forty years of enmity Anthony was ready to unite on nearly any terms the American put forward. The Executive

Committee under Gage, was not as eager and found numerous contentious areas. Especially problematic was the proposal that Stanton, Anthony, and Stone remove themselves from consideration for the presidency of the combined association, as they were considered the causes for the initial split in the first place. This was totally unacceptable and seen as a thinly disguised way to remove Stanton. ". . . neither Mrs. Stone nor Miss Anthony is at present the President of either of these associations. Except for one time Mrs. Stone has never been President of the American . . . They propose that we shall agree to remove our President while they remove a lesser officer."[41] Therefore, at the end of the executive session a counter proposal was approved and sent. Clearly, this Executive Committee felt there was no sense of urgency to rush into any agreement with the American. Instead, the main items in their plan of work for the coming year included the appointment of several committees to report on the actions of each of the political parties and one headed by Harriet Shattuck to work on a recommendation to improve the method of representation within the association to be presented at the next convention. Union was a non-issue.

The real work of the coming year would be influencing the presidential election. Traditionally delegates from NWSA were sent to the political conventions to encourage commitments on woman suffrage from the candidates and a woman suffrage plank in their platform. Results this season, as in the past, were disappointing. The only party offering a nod to woman suffrage was the Prohibition Party, but it came with drawbacks that Stanton had already pointed out and that pitted both Gage and Stanton against Anthony once again. Anthony and May Wright Sewall attended the Republican Convention and interviewed the candidate, Benjamin Harrison. After their interview Anthony wrote to the *Woman's Tribune* that "While the General didn't declare himself in favor of woman's enfranchisement, he expressed great respect for those who are seeking it."[42] Therefore, Anthony threw her support to Harrison.

Frances Willard saw hope for woman suffrage in the platform of the Prohibition Party and its candidate, Clinton B. Fisk. Her contribution to the *Women's Tribune* expressed her "surprise and pain" as she quoted Anthony's letter, "to learn that our dear Miss Anthony 'preferred the

Republican platform to the pernicious doctrine inculcated in the Prohibition Party, that of leaving the inherent right of women to vote . . . to the mercy of the men in the several states, to be voted up or down according to the whim or prejudices of the majority.'" It reads in full:

> That the right of suffrage rests on no more circumstance of race, color, sex or nationality, and that where from any cause, it has been withheld from citizens who are of suitable age and mentality and morally qualified for an intelligent ballot, it should be restored by the people, through the legislatures of the several states, on such educational basis as they may deem wise.[43]

Along with the problem of relying on state legislature, the platform called for moral and educational prerequisites for voters, making it unacceptable to Anthony. Willard saw no problem with such requirements.

Stanton Rusticates; Mayhem Ensues

Stanton was also asked to write her thoughts on the candidates and their platforms. "Although I am rusticating here on the green hills of the Berkshires, yet I cannot maintain a calm, peaceful state of mind, pursued with missives from our co-adjutors, expressing such conflicting views of the political situation." In her usual amusing way, she continued:

> An influential friend called on me while in New York and urged me to use my utmost influence to keep our sisters still, as we have strong friends in both the Republican and Democratic parties, and by word or deed to favor one would make the other hostile. I replied that with the thermometer at 88 "to keep still" would undoubtedly be the most pleasant political position, and one into which I, as an individual, was prone to relapse. However, it is too late to order our cohorts "to keep still" for they are already on the war-path attacking Republicans, Democrats, and Prohibitionists alike.[44]

She concluded that Anthony would support Gen. Harrison and that others "write hopefully" about Fisk. But rather than offer her own analysis of the situation, she enclosed for publication, a private letter, "from my clear sighted friend, Matilda Joslyn Gage [who] expresses fully my own ideas . . ." This is where the wheels come off the wagon. There is no evidence that Stanton asked permission to publish Gage's letter and Stanton probably never gave possible repercussions a thought. Excerpts illustrate that the letter was never meant for publication:

> Miss Anthony says: "If you and the leading women had been at Chicago with headquarters at the Grand Pacific Hotel, we could have gotten the words 'male or female' in the Republican ballot plank, and that not until we go to their conventions in force can we expect anything. Susan is wild on the subject of Republicans – always was. I was very sorry to see your and her pronunciamento in '84 when we had nothing from them. It places our association in a false light. The Democrats were as politic as the Republicans this year, and much more so in '80 when we did have headquarters at one of the first hotels – the Palmer House – with seventy-six delegates who received no consideration, not even as far as the *reception* of our address. The Democrats gave seats among their own delegates to sixteen of ours, placed a committee room in the Opera House at our disposal and Susan . . . was escorted by Carter Harrison to the platform . . . Even the Greenbackers treated us with more respect than the Republicans.
>
> I can never work with the Prohibitionists . . . the first five planks solely concern the liquor traffic; the sixth is on civil service reform; . . . the twelfth, equal wages for equal work to both sexes; eighth, for the abolition of polygamy and the establishment of uniform laws governing marriage and divorce; tenth, for the preservation and defense of the Sabbath as a civil institution . . .
>
> With great inconsistency, while placing suffrage with the states, the Prohibitionists with "the Sabbath," "polygamy," "marriage and divorce," to come under national law, thus turning the body politic feet uppermost.

Gage then inserted the Prohibition plank, in order to describe its weaknesses and writes:

> Here, you see, is no specific mention of women . . . All suffrage is

relegated to the states, with moral and educational qualifications, the "moral" evidently to be twisted church-wise.

I should like to knock together the Republican and Democratic parties and sink them both forever. I am of your opinion, and Mrs. Wallace's that it is a derogation of dignity to appear more or again to the Republicans, and so felt over Susan's Chicago pronunciamentos.

Returning to the Prohibition Party:

> The New York convention was held in Syracuse not long since and battle occurred . . . You should have seen some of the delegates – Methodist brethren, too holy to exist. Another thing which makes this party one of *extreme danger* is the WCTU upon which the Prohibition Party depends for success. Mrs. Chandler in an open letter to Miss Willard . . . declared its belief in Christ as the "author and head of government," who should be recognized in all party platforms. Six or more state conventions have since endorsed this resolution . . .
>
> This looks like a return to the middle ages and proscription for religious opinions and is the *great danger of the hour* . . .
>
> The great dangerous organization of the movement is the WCTU; and Frances Willard, with her magnetic force, her power of leadership, her desire to introduce religious tests into the government, is the most dangerous person upon the American continent today. The Council opened my eyes as never before. I am glad, oh, so glad that Susan does not favor the Prohibition Party. I have hope for her yet, although she does not see the *real* danger.
>
> You and I must stand firm; we have a great tide to stem, and a great battle yet before us. Get ready for a strong fight.[45]

The most telling indicator that Gage did not write this letter for publication or give her consent that it be published is in her use of Anthony's first name. This was simply not done in any published works issued by the NWSA in any format. Further, the candor of the remarks sets it apart from any other of Gage's published works. Far from being reluctant to state her views candidly, she always did, but when she did, she always followed the forms for publishing them, such as, using "Miss Anthony" rather than "Susan." There is no record of Gage's private reaction to finding her letter to Stanton published and she did not respond to the controversy it stirred until September, when she reiterated her point and offered an expanded explanation for her position. Anthony's reaction, however, was immediate. Angry with Gage for writing it and Stanton for sending it, and Clara Colby, Editor of the *Women's Tribune* for publishing it, she wrote to "Dear St. Frances."

> I am more vexed than I can tell you that Mrs. Stanton should send that wretched scribble of Mrs. Gage's to her to the Women's Tribune, and I am chagrined that Mrs. Colby should publish it . . . It is too idiotic for anything. It is complimentary to you in comparison to its fling at "Susan" the vulgar way in which she calls me "Susan" and jibes my lack of sight and insight!! Well you and I can stand it, but the NWSA platform is not agnostic anymore than it is Roman Catholic or Methodist . . . and it is on this point that both Mrs. G and Mrs. S are at fault it seems to me.
>
> They to my face charge me with having become weak and truckling not only to the church women but also to society women! They say I am eaten up with desire to make our movement popular.[46]

By the following issue of the *Women's Tribune* letters maintaining that "Gage was right" and "Gage was wrong" commanded the letters section, and the issue continued to be debated throughout the autumn. Forced to defend herself from the charges of Stanton and Gage, Anthony simply repudiated her own earlier analysis of the temperance women, revealing that she was either so taken with "St. Frances" that she refused to see the danger in the WCTU's support for branding the Constitution with their "Christian" stamp, had forgotten the forty years of church antagonism toward the woman suffrage movement's quest for expanded rights for women, or had truly never seen the wisdom of a secular republic. Stanton's and Gage's arguments for women's civil rights from the first had been grounded in their determination to remove canon law from the civil law with regard to women while Anthony was careering headlong into an alliance with women who wanted to intrude canon law still further into the laws of the land; indeed, into the very foundation of the laws of the republic, the Constitution.

The International Council made Gage aware of the extent to which the WCTU was not only regressive but also dangerous. She and Stanton had long ago analyzed women's position *vis à vis* the laws as they applied to women and consistently found that where and when religious dogma had civic sway, women were diminished, often fatally so. Uniting with the American and its large WCTU membership was unthinkable to Gage. Rather than to surrender, she chose to fight Anthony, to try to save the heart of the National and if not win, at least be defeated with her integrity intact. Perhaps it was time to think seriously about the anti-church organization she and Stanton had talked about for years.

The question that then arises is, why, given her opposition to uniting the two associations, did she fail to attend the Washington Convention in 1889. As the Chair of the Executive Committee she should have been there, and the National should have extended her the means with which to make the trip, as was usual for officers of the association. Anthony had known for years that Gage's financial situation was precarious since the death of her husband, and even before that, she was not a wealthy woman. At the time of the convention she was visiting her children in Dakota Territory and the extra distance made expense money even more necessary. The exact amount offered is unknown. In her notes on the convention Harriet Shattuck says only, ". . . she was not encouraged to go and only a small part of her expenses was offered to be paid. Susan treated her as shabbily as she did me and more so."[47] Anthony had good reason to prevent Gage from attending. She had received a new proposal for union from the American and Gage's presence would certainly have delayed, if not prevented, any final action and Anthony wanted no further delay.

Unaware of the new proposal from the American, and angry over the skimpy financial support offered to her, Gage weighed the possibility that the issue of union would be addressed, let alone finalized, and decided she would not attend. At best, given NWSA's usual procedures, if the topic of the union came up it would be discussed and recommendations made to the membership. They would then need time to discuss and question the particulars before voting on it. Therefore, the earliest timeframe for finalizing the decision would be the following year.

But NWSA's usual procedures were discarded in 1889. As Gage later noted in her *Statement of Facts*, "although the call stated that the subject of union was to come up again, it did not give the convention or a small committee of it, the right to 'unite' without the individual consent of the members; still less did it authorize an entire change in the Constitution."[48] As Chair of the Executive Committee she should have been sent a copy of the American's latest proposal, notified if substantive action on union was imminent, and travel expenses covered and she was not. Had NWSA's usual procedures been followed it would not have been so critical that she attend. On the other hand, since the feat was accomplished long after the majority of women had left the convention, there is reason to suspect that even if she had been in attendance, the deed would have been done after she left.

This was the same strategy used when the NWSA was founded. Then the founders waited until the Massachusetts contingent left the last AERA convention before meeting to create their association.

May Wright Sewall in Charge?

Notes taken by Harriette Robinson Shattuck during and after the Executive Sessions of 1889 describe the usurpation of power by Anthony with the support of her "ring." The first step in the takeover of '89 was for Anthony to assume the right to preside at all three Executive Committee sessions, ". . . as she supposed no one would question her right . . ." She then immediately appointed a new committee to make recommendations on union to the Executive Committee by the third session, less than two days away. At the second session they rejected the work of the Committee on the Basis of Representation, chaired by Shattuck, and adopted instead an entirely new constitution and set of by-laws, that "destroyed the basis of representation . . . and the right of voting [was] taken away from individual members."[49]

At the third session, held between 8:00 and 11:30 p.m. on the last night of the convention after most of the members had already left, the recommendation to unite was unveiled, discussed, and ratified. This was a really busy group! And, what was most unsettling about their work was their strenuous efforts to prevent their membership from voting.

"Clara Colby of Nebraska," according to Harriette Shattuck's' notes, "moved that the vote on union be tabulated by a circular letter to every National member and answers received by a certain date determined by the vote of the NWSA." Shattuck supported Colby arguing that, ". . . she considered the idea embodied in Colby's motion the only fair way that 'otherwise Mrs. Stanton, Mrs. Gage, and other old workers would have no voice' and three times HRS insisted on 'their right to vote.' The union cabal opposed this violently on the grounds, first, that they were 'sent here to vote for the members,'" and, second, that it would stir up the question everywhere while most people did not know there was division."50

May Wright Sewall opposed Colby's suggestion because, "It would be unconstitutional for members to vote by the constitution [they had] just adopted." Shattuck was furious as she had "taken the precaution to ask when this [the new constitution] was to go into effect and Anthony had declared 'at the next annual meeting.'" In a comment written in the margin on Sewall's contradiction of Anthony, Shattuck's mother, Harriet Robinson Shattuck added "How the mighty have fallen!"

In effect, without notification to the membership, many of whom had just left the convention unaware of the constitutional change, voting rights had been dramatically altered. Without their consent to such a change, their right to consent was stripped from them. Shattuck was certain she knew why: "The real reason was that many letters had been received, the majority of which were opposed to union and they knew they had less chance of carrying their point by all voting openly."

The discussion on these points convinced Shattuck that "the advocates for union had combined together and agreed to support each other." They were, she concluded, "afraid to submit the question to the vote of all." Union passed in committee by a vote of 30 to 11. The ring was: Sewall, Anthony, Avery, Johns, Shaw, Blake, Howell, Harker, and Clay." Shattuck's explanation of the vote states that a few who voted for the union were "new workers who desired union, for the sake of the work in their own states, honestly, and [did] not understand the situation." For her, those women were not culpable. But she had venomous words for Sewall and boldly questioned Anthony's leadership:

> Avery's [Rachel Foster] position (who was really opposed) is explained by the two facts that Anthony wanted union and Sewall was determined to have it. Avery is under Sewall's domination . . . and the case is true of Anthony, who, while honestly desiring to do right and best was so blinded by Sewall (that unprincipled schemer and self seeker) that she was unjust in some individual cases and sacrificed not only herself (put her head in a bag, which she had a right to do) but also all other loyal Nationals to this wish to conciliate the Americans. <u>She sold us out and Sewall managed it all</u>.[51]

For Shattuck, the future did not look promising. "I anticipate," she wrote at the end of the sessions, "nothing but the worst results from this patched up union. The best women will have nothing to do with it I am sure." And she felt ". . . sorry for the downfall of Susan. She had joined forces with the enemy and sacrificed not only herself but all the rest of us . . . and so far as I am concerned she is a lost leader. She can and has abandoned us but no power of hers can make us follow her. The Constitution is of the regular Sewallian pronunciamento sort. And binds every member to do, I should judge, just as the officers direct."[52]

This view of Anthony's role in the sessions on union certainly calls into question her leadership at this point. She may have moved away from her dependence on Stanton for advice and "thunderbolts," but neither did she forge an independent, coherent, political agenda. It seems, instead, that she identified the *zeitgeist* and adopted it. In fact, the less she was inspired by Stanton and Gage for her political perspective and the more she was influenced by Willard and Sewall, the more obviously shallow her veneer of "National" ideals became in her eagerness to please her new associates. And this should be no surprise. After all, her initial enthusiasm for woman suffrage was an enthusiasm for Elizabeth Cady Stanton.[53] How quickly she stood aside and abandoned the principle inherent in the "consent of the governed" when Sewall argued that the members should not vote because "they knew nothing about the division and it ought not be stirred up."[54] How could women possibly be trusted to vote on issues of national importance, if they were incapable of judicious voting within their own suffrage organization?

Immediate Protests

During the months following the convention Gage was asked to lead a protest against the union and to force a vote of the members. For this she wrote and circulated "A Statement of Facts" among the NWSA membership. The main issues were:

> . . . the call for the Convention contained no mention that the Constitution – upon which "union" was based – would be revised.

> . . . absent members were not given the right to an expression of an opinion upon the important subject of union.

> . . . because the committee to whom the subject was referred was a packed committee, members who voted "union" thus dictated to many hundreds of thousands of members.

> . . . because grave and momentous questions decided in such a manner are not permanently settled.

> . . . because we believe the National Association would do better work separately and by strictly holding to its former methods.[55]

Especially galling was the fact that the American Woman Suffrage Association conducted itself more honorably. "Let us note," the protest read, "the different method adopted by the American . . . in regard to its own members. By a resolution passed at the AWSA [convention] . . . such a change of Constitution as might be recommended by a majority of the representatives . . . and afterwards accepted by a majority vote of the members . . . was to be accepted; and the Secretary was authorized to take the vote of the members . . . by mail.[56]

Walking it Back

Two months after the convention Anthony responded to the furor over the new Constitution in a letter to Lillie Devereux Blake. She had, "never seen a copy of the new constitution, except as printed in the *Women's Tribune*."

By now she finally noticed that, "there are several defective points in it. 1st that Honorary v-p's shall have <u>no vote</u> so that when you and I are retired to that list we shall not have even a <u>poor one vote</u>! 2. that the <u>direct dollar</u> members have no representation . . ."[57] After vigorously campaigning for its adoption, she was beginning to appreciate the problems with it pointed out by Shattuck and others in the executive session. So great was her enthusiasm to act, she had acted unwisely. The American, in the meantime had not contacted her as to whether or not their members had voted in favor of the union. "I hear nothing of the <u>Boston</u> steps – I wonder if they are taking any toward the closing up of the union!!"

To Olympia Brown, who also circulated the "Statement" she attempted to portray herself as more tolerant that Stanton or Gage; [they say] ". . . because I am not as <u>in</u>tolerant of the so-called <u>Christian women</u> as they, that therefore I have gone, or am about to go over, to the popular church . . ."[58] Even her vaunted support for Stanton as President is used here to excuse her actions on union. She implied to Olympia Brown that she didn't trust the Americans. Apparently, she only advocated union in order to give them enough rope to hang themselves, and hang they would when Mrs. Stanton was elected President:

> Of course, what they expected, perchance hoped was that we in our pride of success would refuse to unite with then . . . But I saw from the first that our position of cheerful welcome . . . to be the right attitude. But I do want you and Mrs. Hooker and all the women who know of the true inwardness of the Stone, Blackwell train to be on hand at our next Washington convention to stand firm as a rock for perfect freedom in the union and for Mrs. Stanton as president of it.
>
> I hear even Lucy Stone has brought herself down to being willing at least not to rebel if Miss Anthony should be elected but that she and others will never <u>submit</u> to be <u>under Mrs. Stanton</u> as <u>president</u> and because of this very fact I want the test made at the first moment of the attempted union then if they won't stand it let them secede again. Then will come the odium to them that won't work with the majority. That is all there will be, nothing but reproach for those who go on the "rule or run principle." Now . . . I do not want

you to tell anyone of these thoughts of mine . . .

I feel sure there will come a revolt if Mrs. Stanton is elected, and hence I want them to have a second chance to show themselves to be the ones who won't submit to the wish and will of the <u>majority</u>. I want them caught in their own trap.[59]

As first one, then another of the old National leaders left, were dismissed, repudiated or squeezed out, Anthony continued to inveigh against them, always insisting they weren't willing to submit to the will of the majority. But it's difficult to invoke the will of the majority if the members are not allowed to vote, and in the case of union the women of the National did not. Therefore, at the crucial moment a vote of the NWSA membership could have proven majority support for the union, if it existed; without it, claims that the union was accomplished by smoke and mirrors would continue to circulate and contribute to the series of secessions that plagued the NAWSA throughout its history. The secretive nature of the proceedings also set a precedent for keeping controversy under wraps or forcing it outside the association, thus robbing it of life.[60]

In an interesting twist of events Olympia Brown had actually voted in favor of union in the committee of thirteen appointed by Anthony at the first executive session. However, she soon regretted that vote and was so upset by the maneuvering to effect the union and disenfranchise the members that she joined Gage in protesting the entire affair. Anthony, who always wanted everything to go her way but smoothly, attempted to convince Brown that she was sure the American would never stand for union on her terms and that was what she had in mind all along. Brown was not convinced, nor was anyone else.

This was not the first time Anthony had used high-handed tactics and then tried to smooth the troubled waters. Stone and Blackwell never believed it was either a coincidence or an oversight that the meeting that resulted in the formation of the National in 1869, just after they left New York, was held only for socializing and then spontaneously became an organizing session for a woman suffrage association. They always felt they had been purposely excluded. But Anthony, always cognizant of the advantages of the public gesture, ignored their angry denunciations and attended the first meeting of their rival American association organized a few months after the perceived snub and had the nerve to ask them to abandon their association and come and join the National. Her long held animosity towards "Little Lucy," "Her Ladyship," and "St. Lucy" had its beginnings in Lucy Stone's justifiable "no thank you."

Little came of the protest by Gage, Brown, Charlotte Daley, Marietta Bones, Shattuck and Robinson. The majority of the NWSA had apparently reached a sufficiently bovine state that they reverently mooed along wherever Anthony led them; and Anthony led them wherever Sewall and Avery wanted her to go. Stanton was right when she said,

> The National Association has been growing politic and conservative for some time. Lucy and Susan alike see suffrage only. They do not see woman's religious and social bondage. Neither do the young women in either association, hence they may as well combine for they have one mind and one purpose.[61]

Unfortunately, even most of the women who were stirred by the protest did, without much trouble, fall in line and remain loyal to Anthony and join the NAWSA. This too was an ominous sign for a political institution. Unselfconsciously they celebrated the change from a political association to a fan club with a gala birthday party for Anthony immediately prior to the first NAWSA convention.

Response to Gage's *Statement of Facts* was not, however, entirely negative. Other women felt as strongly as Gage about the dangerous influence of the WCTU and similar organizations. To draw that influence into the woman suffrage camp was unthinkable for them also. Therefore, Gage felt the time had finally come to organize a liberal, anti-church association to provide the necessary antidote. In October, with the NAWSA convention looming on the horizon she contacted Stanton, among others, expecting and receiving her support. Stanton wrote that she had discussed the matter with Helen Gardener and they had concluded that "there was more to be said in favor than against." She then asked, "How might it be to fight the battle <u>within</u> the suffrage lines, claiming that we have the same right to vote in the church as in the state. Claim one session for this branch, thus avail ourselves of suffrage audiences and finances. I do not know that this is feasible but the thought suggests itself. We might call it the Liberal Suffrage League." Stanton could see that the "suffrage movement languishes today because the newcomers and many of the old ones are afraid to take an advance step." Although, as usual, she was not interested in raising money or organizing, she did promise, "I will speak and give the highest truth I see on all religious and social questions but I will not take any office in any organization. Once out of my present post in the suffrage movement I am a free lance to do and say what I choose and shock people as much as I please."62 The details she would leave to Gage.

By early November Gage wrote enthusiastically to her son T.C. that she had been introduced to some wealthy friends of a Judge Stewart of Rochester, Will T. and Josephine Cables Aldrich of Alabama. She described their meeting at a "fine dinner with seven courses and cham-pagne to drink" but admitted, ". . . what I especially cared for and suited me best was they furnish me the money to commence my work to hold a convention in Washington this winter."63 By January she was deeply involved in the myriad details conventions always required, reserving sleeping rooms and a private parlor for receptions, securing speakers and preparing speeches, writing resolutions, arranging transportation and advertising the public sessions. She decided another newspaper was also necessary and began publishing *The Liberal Thinker* in order to be "in correspondence with people in widely different parts of the country."

The first convention of the Woman's National Liberal Union was scheduled for February 24 and 25, 1890, at Willard's Hall, three days after the close of the first NAWSA convention. "Susan and Blackwell counsel or forbid attendance upon my convention," she reported, but the women came anyway and the convention was a rousing success, attracting all the usual denunciations from pulpit and press to which the National had become a stranger and the NAWSA would never know. Many of the women, to be sure, were cross-overs from the NAWSA convention, including Gage! February was a busy month for suffrage women. Gage not only organized and presided at her own convention but was a featured speaker at the Anthony birthday gala, speaking on "Miss Anthony as Fellow Worker," and attended the NAWSA convention. Conversely, even though Anthony was angry with Gage over the letter published the previous August, thought her convention was "too horrible for anything," and suspected her of spreading rumors that she was trying to supplant Mrs. Stanton, she approved her as a speaker at her birthday party and announced at the NAWSA convention that she had,

> ... made life members of myself, nieces Lucy E. and Louise, and Mrs. Stanton. Now I intend to make Mrs. Minor, Olympia Brown, Phoebe Couzins and Matilda Joslyn Gage life members. I had thought of others, but these last four are of longer standing, were identified with the old National and have suffered odium and persecution because of adherence to it.[64]

Anthony's command of the public gesture was such that it would not have been surprising if she had actually attended the WNLU convention, just as she had the first AWSA convention. What was surprising, however, was that Stanton did not. Stanton had given Gage significant encouragement and promised to speak, but apparently had second thoughts. Two weeks after her letter to Gage, she wrote to Clara Colby saying, "It seems to me that just as we have accepted the offer of union of the two national associations, it would not be possible for me as president of one to take part in immediately organizing another without even making the experiment for one year to see how we can work together." She simply didn't feel that there were enough women and money to maintain a separate association. She concluded, "I would fain do all I can to make the union of the two forces a success. It seems desirable to me from every standpoint. It is time enough a year hence to organize a Liberal League if the experiment of union fails."[65]

Gage, however, was not aware that Stanton had changed her mind until she arrived in Washington. Stanton, by that time had also capitulated to Anthony's need to have her elected to the NAWSA presidency; her letters on Stanton's behalf started immediately upon the close of the preceding year's convention. It is also possible that when she agreed to speak at Gage's convention, she had no idea Gage intended to organize and hold a convention within four months. "Mrs. Stanton behaved the worst of them all." Gage wrote to her son upon hearing that Stanton was willing to let her name stand for election to the presidency of NAWSA before leaving for Europe a week before she was scheduled to speak at her convention. When questioned about the WNLU Convention and the announcements that she was to speak, Stanton replied, "I could not honorably lend my name or influence to what is in the nature of a secession from the suffrage ranks."[66]

Anthony denounced the WNLU Convention and its resolutions as "ridiculous, absurd, sectarian, bigoted, and too horrible for anything."[67] In fact many women found much to criticize about the newly formed WNLU. Letters in the *Woman's Tribune* from March through the middle of May bristled with indignation over the resolutions against the church and the Christian Party. Parker Pillsbury lamented in April that Gage had lost most of her former friends and co-workers of forty years. They had "almost, if not quite without exception . . . abandoned her and cast her out even her name as an unclean thing."[68]

However, the break among the three long-time associates, friends, and leaders was not so profound as Pillsbury portrayed it, nor very long-lived. Stanton took Gage's convention in stride, ". . . it seemed to go off all right and no one was hurt. How groundless all these fears are about 'hurting the cause.' How we exaggerate the influence of trifles."[69]

As far as the "perfect harmony" that Anthony proclaimed union would bring, it was an ephemera. After only a few days company with the AWSA, Stanton feared that "we shall always have trouble with Blackwell and Lucy. You see they make a point of contradicting what I say . . . But we shall see in due time I am afraid, we made a mistake when we took them in as even partners." Henry Brown Blackwell was the main problem. Stanton called him an "autocratic hag" and Anthony, somewhat more optimistically thought, ". . . the union is in working trim – and if only HBB's tongue and pen could be kept from harping upon the causes of their old secession all would go as merry as May." But his tongue and pen were not stilled. Instead he began printing a series of articles on the Kansas campaign of 1869, distorting events and infuriating Stanton. "He is bound to pitch with me. He does not mention you [Anthony] because it is his policy to play you off against me. Just what I told you they would do if I was made President. Now . . . am I to keep silent and let Blackwell go on with his lies and insults . . . ?" Out of patience, Stanton took aim at the reports of the NAWSA convention, too. In a letter to Clara Colby she said:

> I never did hear such twaddle. Where were you and Susan? . . . May Wright Sewall's discussion was simply ridiculous in her position and who did comprise the Committee on Resolutions? They read as if they had been thrown together on the way to the hall. That twaddle about Christ sounds like that rattle-brained Mrs. Bennett. I should think you and Susan would feel ashamed of the Resolutions and that discussion. I am I assure you.[70]

Union, in fact, did not guarantee harmony; it did not create broad support for woman suffrage, instead it attracted new enemies in the form of the liquor interests and among recent immigrants, now that the entire spectrum of woman suffrage advocates were associated with the platform of the WCTU, and it certainly did not reinvigorate the woman suffrage movement.

This research is not, however, intended as an indictment of the effectiveness of the union. In fact, the eventual uniting of the two associations was probably inevitable, given the trends of the time period. Anthony could have relied on those trends, followed standard NWSA procedures, and outvoted Gage and the others. The results would have remained the same, but her reputation would have remained above reproach. Her ends did not justify her means.

By 1885 it was becoming obvious even with the NWSA that the days of radical resolutions were fading. That year the resolutions against the "dogmas incorporated in the religious creeds derived from Judaism . . . teaching that woman was an afterthought . . . her sex a misfortune . . . maternity a curse" and resolving ". . . these dogmas are an insidious poison . . ." were introduced and advocated by Stanton. Anthony argued against consideration of them saying that, "Settling any question of human rights by people's interpretations of the Bible is never satisfactory." She was joined by others and the resolutions tabled. The following year a similar resolution from Stanton elicited more strong discussion. Many did not feel that "the churches are our greatest enemies. They may have been so in Mrs. Stanton's early days but today they are our best helpers." This time the resolution passed 32 yeas to 24 nays but there was obviously a growing antipathy toward resolving such issues within the suffrage association. Helen Gougar spoke for many when she said, ". . . this association is for suffrage and not for the discussion of religious dogmas."[71] The American public at large was becoming more conservative and so were the women of the National. Therefore, a vote on the issue of union would have passed, if not in 1889, then in 1890 or 1891. Neither Gage nor Stanton could have stemmed that tide or its results.

Anthony Consolidates Her Power

What was to be gained by Anthony in pressing for union in the fashion that she did? She identified the leader of the opposition: Gage, lulled her into a false sense of security, and refused her all but the most meager travel allowance. Then in executive session usurped her position, conspired to refute all arguments to let the members vote, and turned the results into a test of personal loyalty. When she wrote to women around the country to "come and stand by Susan once more," that was all she meant, stand by her personally, not "Susan" as a symbol of some grander ideal. What she gained was power.

From the time of the union until her death, Anthony controlled absolutely the reins of power in the NAWSA. Even after her death, it took NAWSA a decade to replace the ineffective Anna Howard Shaw, Anthony's chosen successor, with the dynamic Carrie Chapman Catt.

Gage, however, was only one of several pioneer workers who felt the sting of Anthony's tactic. The eclipse of Stanton and Gage, as well as other highly visible NWSA leaders began with Anthony's capture of the NAWSA. Gage's principled exit doomed her to obscurity, but one of the earliest signs that Stanton would suffer the same fate is recorded in the May 17, 1890, *Woman's Tribune*. In an untitled article appearing on page 4 is the news that "There is a movement on foot, inaugurated by Miss Willard, to secure the funds for a portrait bust of Miss Anthony, to be placed in the World's Fair in Chicago." The article indicates it approval of the project but protests, "It would never do to let Miss Anthony stand alone without the companionship of her lifelong friend, . . . Mrs. Stanton. Mrs. Stanton is the founder and mother of the organized work for the enfranchisement of women. She is also older than Miss Anthony and stands today at the head of the united American suffrage hosts." The *Tribune* needed to remind its readers about Stanton only two months after her election. But then the election itself was more about Anthony's power than support for Stanton.[72]

After 1890 Anthony stood more and more alone as the singular face and symbol of woman suffrage. It is no accident that by the turn of the century none of the National's leaders in 1889, save Anthony, were still prominent in either the suffrage ranks, honorable retirement, or its collective memory. Stanton, Gage, Blake, and Duniway, Anthony's equals were replaced by Anthony's "nieces."

The NAWSA's final repudiation of Stanton over the publication of the *Woman's Bible* has been well discussed and Anthony's defense of Stanton generally lauded. What has been less noted was that her defense was not immediate or exhaustive. While claiming to have had nothing to do with either Stanton's *Bible* or the NAWSA's censure, she refused to resign from NAWSA and "leave her half-fledged chicks without a mother." But, let's not overlook the fact that her "half-fledged chicks" had at the time over a decade each of experience in suffrage work. Therefore, her defense of Stanton can readily be seen as another of her many well-timed public gestures. She reprimanded Carrie Catt and Rachel Foster Avery, but accepted their refusal to repent; her position required it.

Another example of Anthony's new power involved Abigail Scott Duniway. In 1889, Duniway was one of the most prominent western suffrage leaders. She too lost status by the mid 1890s as a result of a disagreement with Anthony and her troops. Based on her long experience in the western states, Duniway tried to convince Anthony to keep suffrage and temperance separate in the western campaign. Washington State WCTU leaders had published pronouncements indicating that woman suffrage would lead directly to the "annihilation of the liquor traffic."

Duniway insisted "such sentiments frightened men into voting against equal suffrage." Anthony was unpersuaded and in 1896, "instructed the state leader [Duniway] to stay out of the Idaho suffrage fight [where she had been a leading contender], which would be managed by an eastern organizer." Later Duniway charged that "national leaders, wanting to manage the suffrage campaign 'held a supposedly secret conclave with a few of my ambitious eleventh-hour opponents and decided to take the bull by the horns.'" Duniway also opposed Anthony's powerful control of NAWSA but, "Although Anthony restricted her and eventually played politics against [her] in her own state . . . [she] threw shafts at easier targets, including Colby, Shaw and their Portland allies."[73]

The last of the important old Nationals to fall was New York State Woman Suffrage Association President, Lillie Devereux Blake. Blake had joined NWSA soon after its formation in 1869 and had risen to prominence through both her state and national work. One day after the 1899 NAWSA convention in Grand Rapids, Michigan, she was notified by the Business Committee, through Carrie Catt, that Anthony had disbanded Blake's Legislative Committee. The Business Committee had no authority to take such an action and Blake protested the move only to discover that Anthony had replaced her committee with a committee of one, Laura M. Johns. Blake had chaired the Legislative Committee for five years and hoped the Convention would overturn the high-handed action of disbanding her committee, but such was Anthony's power, the decision stood. Stanton, who had already felt the sting of repudiation, sympathized with her:

> You have not been treated by our young coadjutors with less con-
> sideration than I have been. They refused to read my letters and
> resolutions . . . they have denounced the *Woman's Bible* unsparingly
> . . . Because of this hostile feeling I renounced the presidency and
> quietly accept the situation . . . Now you must do the same.[74]

Blake, however, made one last attempt to regain her position within the NAWSA when Anthony announced she would retire in 1900. Many who were angered by the action of Anthony and the other members of the Business Committee felt Blake's long years of service deserved recognition. Therefore, she was encouraged to run for the presidency. Her petition was signed by Stanton, Dr. Mary Putnam Jacobi, and M. Olivia Sage, all prominent members of the organization. She soon realized, however, that she did not have the support necessary to win against Anthony's choice, Carrie Chapman Catt, and so withdrew her name and as had others before her, left NAWSA.

One of her last contacts with Anthony came when Ida Husted Harper wrote asking for her to write a chapter for the fourth volume of the *History*. She agreed but confided to her diary that "As Miss Anthony is directing its writing; I shall probably have small recognition." Blake's biographer and daughter agreed. "An uninformed person, reading the chapter . . . on the work in New York would be convinced that Miss Anthony was also New York State's leading spirit and that Mrs. Blake's part in the work was negligible."[75] A reading of the chapter confirms this assessment.

In 1903, Anthony commented on Blake's withdrawal from NAWSA in a letter to Gage's daughter, Helen. In her reply to Helen's complaint that her mother had received such slight credit for her many years of work on behalf of NWSA and her work on the *History*, discussed earlier, Anthony wrote:

> Mrs. Blake has become a dead letter to us since 1900; then she aspired to be president instead of Mrs. Catt . . . I have seen her but once since and that was at Mrs. Stanton's funeral. She had only nine votes; she ought to have seen and known her limitations . . . she has chosen to go off in a society called the Legislative League, or something . . . she hasn't been to a single meeting that I know of since 1900. I am sorry for her but bolters always come out at the little end of the horn and she is no exception.[76]

Through this appraisal of Blake's actions, Anthony revealed no comprehension of Blake's reasons for feeling compelled to leave and took no responsibility for it. Because Anthony chose to offer her philosophy on "bolters' to Gage's daughter, we can assume she felt similarly toward Gage.

Gage was only the first of many casualties in the union wars. Rather than an insignificant moment in the history of the woman suffrage movement, an analysis of machinations used and the fallout from the uniting of the two associations lays bare the political Anthony bringing to fruition her years of work to accumulate power into her own hands by organizing a power base among the conservative women who came to dominate the suffrage armies. That Anthony's vision extended no farther than the enfranchisement of women and her philosophy was no deeper than the needs of the moment goes a long way toward explaining the arid agenda of the NAWSA. Anthony created an authoritarian, hierarchical association, devoted to persons not ideals. When in her final moments she "looked intently into Anna's eyes" [Anna Howard Shaw] and made her "promise that you will keep the presidency of the association as long as you are well enough to work," a line of succession was established.[77] In such a system, voting is simply a formality.

We have too long venerated Anthony and too seldom analyzed her as a leader. The executive session that decided union for thousands of NWSA women proved that the suffrage leadership of Anthony loyalists had no faith in suffrage or they would have insisted the members have the right to vote on it. The irony that they were able to do it in spite of protest speaks to how little the membership actually understood the value of enfranchisement. It had become something "out there" that others denied them. They didn't recognize its loss when they agreed to deny it to themselves. Anthony never explained or justified her actions beyond a steadfast reiteration that those who "won't submit to the wish and will of the majority" were "bolters" and it "will come the odium to them that won't work with the majority. That is all there will be, nothing but reproach for those who go on the 'rule or run principle.'"[78] Clearly it never occurred to Anthony that the minority view had any value. But, it is stunning to see how limited her faith in woman suffrage actually was.

Gage's career, however, was far from over when she left NWSA. And, although never quite as comfortable with Anthony and Stanton after the events of 1890, even those relationships were not ended.

NOTES

1. Harper, Ida Husted, *The Life and Work of Susan B. Anthony*, II, 632

2. *Ibid.*, 659

3. Anthony, Susan B. and Ida Husted Harper, *History of Woman Suffrage*, IV, 164.

4. Buhle and Buhle, 31; Flexner, 262; DuBois, 181.

5. Griffith, Elisabeth, *In Her Own Right*, 195, 197

6. Kerr, Andrea Moore, *Lucy Stone, Speaking Out for Equality*, 224-227, SBA Diary, Feb. 17, 1890, Barry, Kathleen, *Susan B. Anthony, A Biography of a Singular Feminist*, 297

7. Barry, 294-299, 401 f.n.'s 47-53.

8. *Ibid.*, 298.

9. *Ibid.*, 299. Anthony did not seek to "redefine or reshape the meaning of womanhood" so much as she sought to give any definition of womanhood the right to vote.

10. *Ibid.*, 299

11. Strom, Sharon Hartman, "Leadership and Tactics in the American Woman Suffrage Movement: A New Perspective from Massachusetts, *Journal of American History*, 302.

12. Wagner, Sally Roesch, "Introduction," Gage, *Woman, Church and State*, xxxv.

13. SBA to Amelia Jenks Bloomer, Oct., 1880?, S-A Papers

14. MJG to Thomas Clarkson Gage, May 26, 1888.

15. ECS to Theodore Weld Stanton, May 21, 1880

16. SBA to Rachel G. Foster, Dec. 13, 1881

17. Blake, Katherine Devereux and Margaret Louise Wallace, *Champion of Women, The Life of Lillie Devereux Blake*, (New York: Fleming H. Revell Co. 1943), 115

18. SBA to Rachel Foster, May 18, 1881

19. *Ibid.*, March ?, 1887

20. *Ibid.*, Oct. 25, 1880 and Oct. 30, 1880

21. *Ibid.*, Dec. 13, 1881

22. ECS to Lillie Devereux Blake, Dec. 30, 1881

23. SBA to Euphemia Fenno Tudor, Jan. 9, 1882.

24. *HWS*, III, 221, 229

25. SBA to Elizabeth Harbert, July 7, 1880

26. *Ibid.*, March 8, 1882

27. SBA to Harriet J. H. Robinson, Oct. 24, 1880

28. SBA to Clara Barton, Sept. 1, 1881

29. SBA to Barbara J. Thompson, Nov. 6, 1881

30. SBA to Elizabeth M. B. Harbert, Dec. 9, 1883

31. MJG to TCG, May 26, 1888

32. ECS to Harriet J. H. Robinson, Sept. 30, 1886

33. SBA to Rachel G. Foster, Ja. 15, 1888

34. MJG to SBA, March before 26th, 1887, SBA to Elizabeth M. Harbert, Feb. 3, 1888

35. SBA to Rachel G. Foster, March, 1887

36. *Liberal Thinker,* Syracuse, N.Y., January 1890, 4
37. *Ibid.*
38. EDs, "A Letter from Mrs. Stanton." *Woman's Tribune,* Jan. 21, 1888, 2. A tiny article tucked away on page 7 of this same issue offers a glimpse of things to come. Laura Johns of the Kansas WSA writes a thank you to the American at Boston for their help raising funds for the Kansas Society at their Boston bazaar. Johns would rise rapidly and become one of the Anthony "ring" confirming union in 1889. She would still later replace a deposed Lillie Devereux Blake.
39. Letters appear in every issue of the *Woman's Tribune* from March to August. See August 18 for Gage's letter calling Frances Willard the "most dangerous person upon the American continent today."
40. Lucy Stone to SBA, Nov. 7, 1887; SBA to Lucy Stone, Dec. 13, 1887; SBA to Elizabeth M. Harbert, Feb. 3, 1868
41. 20 NWSA Washington Convention, Executive Session, April 3-5, 1888.
42. SBA, "Letter from Miss Anthony," *Woman's Tribune,* July 7, 1888
43. Frances Willard, "Symposium of Opinions About Political Parties by Eminent Women," *Woman's Tribune,* August 16, 1888
44. ECS, "Letter from Mrs. Stanton," *Woman's Tribune,* August 18, 1888
45. MJG, "Letter from Mrs. Gage," *Woman's Tribune,* August 18, 1888
46. SBA to Frances Willard, August 23, 1888 and MJG, "Letter from Mrs. Gage," *Woman's Tribune,* Sept., 22, 1888
47. Shattuck, Harriet, "The Union," 33
48. MJG, "Statement of Facts," 4
49. Shattuck, "The Union," 1, and MJG, "Statement of Facts," 1
50. Shattuck, 9-1, 23.
51. *Ibid.,* 14-16
52. *Ibid.,* 31-32
53. Barry, 64-65 and Griffith, 73-74
54. Shattuck, 27
55. MJG, "Statement," 7
56. *Ibid.,* 4-5
57. SBA to Lillie Devereux Blake, March 11, 1889
58. SBA to Olympia Brown, March 11, 1889
59. *Ibid.*
60. DuBois, *Stanton, Anthony,* 181. Gage left, Abigail Scott Duniway was dismissed, Stanton's *Bible* was repudiated and Lillie Devereux Blake squeezed out.
61. ECS to Olympia Brown, May 8, 1888
62. ECS, *Liberal Thinker,* 5
63. MJG to T.C. Gage, Nov. 6, 1889
64. Harper, *The Life,* II, 659 and SBA to May Wright Sewall, Jan. 8, 1890
65. ECS to Clara Colby, Mov. 13, 1889
66. ECS, *Washington Post,* Feb. 9, 1890, in Wagner, "Introduction." xxxvi, *Woman, Church and State*
67. Wagner, "Introduction," and SBA to Lillie Devereux Blake, Feb. 6, 1890; SBA to Eliza Wright Osborn, Feb. 15, 1890 and March 5, 1890.

68. Parker Pillsbury to Lillie Devereux Blake, April 11, 1890 in Wagner, "Introduction."

69. ECS to Clara Colby, March 21, 1890

70. ECS to Clara Colby, March 21, 1890 and ECS to Clara Colby and SBA, June 6, 1890.

71. *HWS,* IV, 58-61; 75-77

72. *Woman's Tribune,* May 17, 1890, 4.

73. Edwards, Thomas G. *Sowing Good Seeds, The Northwest Suffrage Campaigns of Susan B. Anthony,* (Portland, Oregon: Oregon Historical Society Press, 1990) 165, 251, 303.

74. ECS to Lillie Devereux Blake, June 14, 1899 in Blake, Katherine Devereux and Margaret Louis Wallace, *Champion of Women, The Life of Lillie Devereux Blake,* (New York: Fleming H. Revell Co., 1943) 200

75. *Ibid.,* 210-211.

76. SBA to Helen Leslie Gage, July 30, 1903.

77. Barry, 355

78. SBA to Olympia Brown, March 11, 1889; SBA to Helen Leslie Gage, July 30, 1903.

CHAPTER 5

Her Magnum Opus:
Woman, Church, and State

A FTER nearly forty years of working together, the rupture between Anthony, Stanton, and Gage was marked by rancor and recrimination all around. Anthony thought Gage's "bolting" was "too horrible for anything." Stanton characterized it as a "secession from the suffrage ranks." Gage summed up their behaviors as "despicable." But, in spite of these initial responses they each remained mindful of each other. Gage and Stanton, in fact, eventually collaborated on the *Woman's Bible*. Gage's reconciliation with Anthony was never as complete as it was with Stanton, but then Anthony had always had difficulty with Gage's independence. Whereas Stanton usually took a ho hum attitude toward Anthony's enthusiasms for new flames in the suffrage ranks, Gage was more than a little critical of them. She had voiced her disdain toward Anthony's "chicks" and saw Willard as one of the most dangerous people in the country. Up to the last, Gage continued to cast a skeptical eye on Anthony's overtures in spite of an obvious desire to be part of, at the very least, honorably retired elders. But, even partial reconciliations would have to wait for time sufficient to the healing process.

As has been discussed, the conventions of 1890, both NAWSA and WNLU, marked significant moments in the woman suffrage vs. women's rights movement. For Gage, two important revelations marked the year 1890 as a significant turning point in her career. The first offered insight into the years still left to travel before woman suffrage would be accomplished. The second supported her decision to leave the NAWSA.

Both encouraged a kind of freedom of thought and action she had not known before.

The first revelation came on the heels of yet another defeat for woman suffrage, this time in South Dakota. In an article prepared for the *Woman's Tribune* she discussed the reasons for the suffrage amendment's defeat and predicted:

> The sense of abstract justice seems to be dormant in most persons, men or women. To do a thing simply because it's right . . . does not seem to be the aim of most people. With fuller experience I became assured that some great political necessity must first arise before the large majority of men could be made to act in her favor, some emergency as serious as that which endowed colored men.[1]

With no political necessity or national emergency in the offing she allowed other issues and interests to command her attention. "Since January 1st I have written or finished up "The Esotericism of the National Flag," "The Influence of Food upon Character," "Air as Treatment," and "Food as Medicine," she advised her daughter Helen, and "I am to speak before the West Side Vegetarian Society next Wednesday." She began painting again and pursued a life-long interest in astrology and the occult sciences.

In her second, more profound revelation she decided the church's antagonism toward women's equality and its belief in the inferiority of woman was not incidental to its teachings but the very foundation of its beliefs. From that basis all its other teachings derived. As she told the story to her son,

> I did not at first think of attacking the foundations of the church itself, but I was thinking one day when a sudden light came into my mind, an illumination, which said "the church" and then I knew it was right.
>
> I thought it all carefully over and I knew I meant the <u>church</u> itself and I said so. . . . I am as much as ever a believer in the invisible church but not in this rotten thing known in the world as "the Christian Church."

If because there are four hundred and fifty million Christians in the world (which I doubt) is a sign of a grain of truth, Buddhism which numbers twice as many and heathendom are all "signs."[2]

This thesis, first expressed publicly in her speech to the WNLU convention, "The Dangers of the Hour," also articulated her belief that ". . . wherever we find laws of the state bearing with greater hardship upon woman than upon man, we shall ever find them due to the teachings of the church." For Gage, the church's main access to power was through its laws on marriage and education which required "the ignorance and degradation of women." She continued:

> Its control over woman in the two questions of marriage and education have given it keys of power more potent than those of Peter. With her uneducated, without civil or political rights, the church is sure of its authority . . . regarding her having brought sin into the world.[3]

Her analysis, however, was not limited to the teachings of the Catholic Church. ". . . Catholics are scarcely more greedy for power over this relation [marriage] than are Protestants . . . Episcopalians, Congregationalists, Presbyterians and other sects."[4] Gage always held up to ridicule the practices and pronouncements of priests and ministers; "boxing them around with their own theology." Free now of the demands of the National she began her most important writing.

Woman, Church & State

Woman, Church and State stands alone. Although the suffrage movement moved on words; through its speeches, newspapers, petitions, resolutions, and more, *Woman, Church and State* is the only monograph written by a nineteenth century suffragist. Susan Mosher Stuard's recent analysis, "Matilda Joslyn Gage Writes a World History of Women," refers to Gage as a "pioneer" who:

> . . . aspired to compose a history as methodologically rigorous as her scholarly models. Gage formulated a mode of analysis adopted by many later feminist scholars . . . she came to divergent conclusions

by turning her lens toward woman's condition. In other words, Matilda Joslyn Gage qualifies as a pioneer in the world history movement; in her instance, history with woman's debased condition as central concern in contrast to more typical nineteenth-century histories that tended to feature man's steady progress toward his present eminence.[5]

Women of Gage's generation regularly mined the past for antecedents of heroic proportions to "prove" a variety of female qualities and circumstances. They looked for women of ability, endurance, and bravery as well as examples of women's oppressions. Gage encouraged "Everywoman" to be her own historian, "to read and examine; accept or reject from the proof offered," to think for herself. Moreover, her research "moved beyond what women had accomplished to reasons why the women of whom general histories took note were few and often beleaguered."[6] Her research exemplified this. She was NWSAs recognized authority on important events and people in women's past. Always widely read, she kept voluminous files of research materials. She was trained in Latin, Greek, and French and well versed in the Bible. "No one," she wrote to her son, "can judge in regard to it [the Bible] without having read it. I read it through before I was nine years old and have read it more or less ever since."[7]

Gage's own learnedness compelled her to a lifelong examination of woman's role in society. Her speeches frequently focused on some aspect of her current researches rather than adhering to strictly woman suffrage arguments. After all, they had been done to death and had little pizzazz left. A few of her titles include "Woman in Ancient Egypt," "The Basis of Immorality in Christian Countries," "Queen Esther," "Was Woman an Afterthought?" and "The Feminine Principle in Nature."[8] She and other feminists quickly identified religious dogma as the root of their disabilities. Certainly, some of the most strenuous attacks on their reform came from the churches. It was a rare denomination that welcomed woman's rights. ". . . Universalists, Unitarians, and some non-evangelical Congregationalists unofficially supported the integration of women into their established ministries and numbered among their members a high proportion of male feminists." The Quakers, of course, had always included women as equal members.[9] In spite of these small inroads in main-line churches, the vast majority of churches regularly used woman suffrage as a reliable tool to whip their members into a froth against it and in favor of the maintenance of the *status quo*, which they implied had been immutable truth since the beginning of time.

It was against this backdrop that she published *Woman, Church and State*. With it she intended to disprove the myth "that God designed the subjection of woman, and yet that her position has been higher under Christianity than ever before." And, she wanted to inspire women to "read history for themselves and having read it, dare to draw their own conclusions from its premises. Her arguments on both the "fall" and Christianity's supposed elevation of woman are shaped by the issues of her era yet bear the imprint of her historical perspective. Her evidence of the universality of woman's suffering under Christianity is arrayed to advocate change, but NOT a return to an idealized past.[10]

Woman is unique among the "histories" written by the 19th-century suffragists. Most of the works called histories were actually laundry lists of famous women of the past and present. Most had a moral, an injustice to lament, or a "good example" to follow. Others, were the cut and paste type, like the *HWS*. Other than the essays by Gage and Stanton, and a few other writers, the *HWS* is essentially a compilation of NWSA ephemera. And, even though much of it is a cut and paste volume, it gains a large part of its value from its rich trove of documents that would otherwise be lost to us. A reminiscence like Stanton's *Eighty Years and More* offers lively reading but can't be taken seriously as a reliable source. Unlike these types of volumes, *Woman* sustains a thesis throughout, offers evidence to support its thesis, and documents its sources. And, although grounded in its own time, the issues argued are remarkably current, anticipating the important issues of the 20th- and 21st-century's woman's rights movement.[11]

In 1886, with work on Volume III of the *HWS* finished Stanton and Gage began organizing their decades-long research on the imposition of the church into women's lives. Stanton was inspired by the publication of the Church of England's new revision of the Bible in

1881 to gather together a group of like-minded women to produce a Bible revised according to woman's insights into its texts. "The object," she declared in the Preface is "to revise only those texts and chapters directly referring to women, and those also in which women are made prominent by their exclusion." Stanton, Gage, and the other members of the committee began their exegesis intending to demonstrate its contradictions, to challenge Christianity's claim of divinity, and to discredit its brand of morality. As Stanton explained in her Introduction to Part I, "When in the early part of the Nineteenth century, women began to protest against their civil and political degradation, they were referred to the Bible for an answer. When they protested against their unequal position in the church, they were referred to the Bible. This led to a general and critical study of the Scriptures."[12] It was never a mystery why women's civil rights were truncated, what was a mystery was why, in a nation professing the separation of church and state, the Bible had any bearing on it. Reading for themselves and interpreting for themselves was one way to resist the pronouncements from the pulpits.

As supportive of Stanton's work as Gage was, she was at the same time ready to plunge into her own work on *Woman, Church and State*. She began by notifying T.C. "I am one of the committee of corresponders for the *Woman's Bible* revision and Chair of the Historical Committee . . . Mrs. Stanton's wishing me to write the introduction. I first want to get off *WC&S* and then I shall feel at liberty [to help Mrs. Stanton]." *Woman* first appeared in an abbreviated form as Chapter XV of Volume I of the *HWS*. Anthony had argued against its inclusion but Gage was pleased with the generally good notices it received. Especially pleasing was a note from pioneering reform journalist, Jane Swisshelm of the former Pittsburgh *Saturday Visitor*, a "racy reform paper issued from 1848-1857." Swisshelm declared it "the most valuable part of the Woman Suffrage History." Gage was now eager to complete her work.[13]

It is possible to see the influence of both Evangelical Protestantism and Freethought Doctrine in her work. It was in large part the needs of the Evangelical clergy and the cult of domesticity that had together shaped the public role of women in the moral crusades of the Second Great Awakening. She argued against both. The clergy proclaimed:

Women have a work to do in the House of God, Presbyterian Matthew Perrine told the first annual meeting of the Female Missionary Society for the Poor of the City of New York and its Vicinity in 1817. Domesticity dominated Perrine's discussion of how "pious females . . . may greatly assist the public ministers . . . female hands shall be employed in the finest needlework to adorn the Church for her presentation to the King."[14]

The legacy of this era "was not a conclusion to the question of woman's appropriate social and religious role but rather a vigorous opening of the questions itself." Women like Gage and Stanton interpreted the reform atmosphere of the antebellum years as an opportunity to expand woman's role to the fullest extent of human endeavor. Their experiences as abolitionists and woman suffrage reformers led them to explorations into the foundations of woman's disabilities: Christianity itself.

In part because of the excesses of evangelical zeal during the early part of the 19th century, a countervailing resurgence of freethought found staunch allies. Gage grounded her examination of what she referred to as "churchianity" in this philosophy." She was well versed in freethought. Her father was a freethinker and had always encouraged her to think for herself. "He was more to me than most colleges are to students for he taught me to investigate and not to fear public opinion – but to think for myself – a great and wonderful education."[15]

Well-known members of upstate New York reform circles, her parents raised Gage in an atmosphere of free inquiry. The upstate area itself was known for its liberal reforms, attracting alike evangelicals, spiritualists, and experiments in communal living such as the Oneida Community and a short-lived freethought community in nearby Skaneateles, New York, from 1843-1846. Freethinkers in the tradition of Thomas Paine, men like George Bethune English, author of *The Grounds of Christianity Examined by Comparing the New Testament with the Old,* and William Munday, author of *An Examination of the Bible* along with socialist freethinkers like Robert Owens, rejected the Bible entirely or in part. English questioned and ultimately rejected the Messiahship of Jesus. Munday objected to the idea that "truth was revealed to any man or set of men . . ." and proved "to his satisfaction that the Bible [did] not serve to benefit humanity." Implicitly and often explicitly the arguments of freethinkers concluded that Christian dogma had retarded not advanced civilization. William J. Bright spoke for most freethinkers when he wrote:

> It is the religion of this land that robs the poor man of his natural right to the soil, and the means of obtaining an honest livelihood for himself and little ones. It is the religion of the American church that robs the bondsman of his inalienable right to himself, his wife, and his children. It is this religion that justifies villainy, allows robbery, and baptizes in the Christian name the blackest enormities that were ever perpetrated by depraved mortals. . . . The people must know that the church is the enemy of human rights, and . . . a brotherhood of thieves, in the fullest sense of the term.16

They weren't kidding around when they took on the church and their harsh language did not go unnoticed. But, they remained undeterred. Their arguments appealed to the Constitution and the rights of man to account for human progress. "Whatever truth Christianity did contain had existed in the book of nature long before the coming of Christ." Gage perfectly echoes Stanton's thoughts in her introduction to Stanton's *Woman's Bible* and applies them specifically to religion's impact on women. "I do not believe that any man ever saw or talked with God, I do not believe that God inspired the Mosaic Code, or told the historians what they say he did about woman, . . . There are some general principles in the holy books of all religions that teach love, charity, liberty, justice, and equality for all the human family . . . whose lustre cannot be dimmed by the false sentiments and vicious characters bound up in the same volume."17

Gage's *Woman, Church, and State* was conceived as a history. In a departure from freethinkers' usual strategy of Biblical exegesis, Gage takes the basic premises of the free thought creed and offers historic documentation to prove the theory's assertions. She also charted new paths by expanding standard freethought ideology to argue its tenets from a feminist perspective. To argue against the notion that God created woman's subjection Gage asserted a state of nature thesis that "the earliest semblance of the family is traceable to the mother and child alone." Woman ". . . was in reality the founder of civilization." Her first chapter, The Matriarchate" explains that as a result of the "great advances in historical knowledge" during the "last half century . . . libraries and manuscripts long inaccessible have been opened to scholars, and the spirit of investigation has made known many secrets of the past, brought many hidden things to light."

The new knowledge evidenced traces of a time when the great institutions of society recognized the creative force of women. Ancient customs still lingering in Java, Australia, and Egypt "prove that woman had acquired great liberty under the old civilizations." Descent "through a common mother preceded that of descent through the father." This priority "controlled the state and indicated the form of religion." She amassed a wealth of evidence to argue that the earliest civilizations were matriarchal. She also argued that Christianity had over time expunged the feminine principle "and the spiritual significance" from its "own most holy words . . . Jehovah . . . signifying the masculine-feminine God."[18]

Once she had dispensed with the idea that Christianity ushered in a better situation for women, she analyzed the increasingly masculinist interpretation of scripture and the accompanying elevation of the male priesthood. Church doctrine "recognizing marriage as a necessity for the continuance of the species" also taught "that woman was under an especial curse and all restrictions placed upon her were . . . just punishment for having caused the fall of man." Because "woman was held to be unclean . . . marriage itself and especially priestly marriage came under increasing fire: "married priests, more than celibates, were believed subject to infestation by demons." The establishment of a celibate priesthood according to Gage opened the doors to a number of consequences.

First: The doctrine of woman's inherent wickedness and close relationship with Satan took on new strength.

Second: Canon Law gained full control of civil law.

Third: An organized system of debauchery arose under the mask of priestly infallibility.

Fourth: Auricular confession was confirmed as a dogma of the church.

Fifth: Prohibition of the Scriptures to the laity was enforced.

Together, Gage argued, these dogmas allowed the church to solidify its power, "holding control over the conscience of men, asserting the power to unlock the doors of heaven and hell . . . in the end prove[d] conqueror, and the foulest crimes against woman receive[d] the approval of the entire Christian world."

Gage traced the insinuation of canon law into the civil code of England and later to the United States, to find the further degradation of woman upheld by the power of both church and state. She found that the power and privileges of the priestly gender were transformed into power and privileges for all males, especially the accumulation of wealth through inheritance, property rights, and educational rights, all of which were denied to women. In her analysis she found that the consequences of Christianity, including the Protestant sects, had a profoundly negative effect on the world. "The Catholic, Greek, and Protestant divisions, all degrade women but under different forms." The myth that "woman's position has been higher under Christianity than ever before" was debunked in her discussion of women's safety and work. "Each great division of Christianity alike proclaims the supreme sinfulness of woman in working for the elevation of her sex. That the women of every Christian land fear to meet a man in a secluded place by day or by night, is of itself sufficient proof of the low state of Christian morality." In Christian lands, "we find woman has chiefly been regarded as an element of wealth; the labor of wife and daughters, the sale of the latter into the prostitution of a loveless marriage, having been a universally extended form of domestic slavery." And in the waged labor force, "for the same kind of work men are paid three times more wages than are paid to women." Middle aged women find it impossible to secure employment, "the woman of middle life is the least regarded in her efforts for a livelihood. The reason remains the same. Looked upon during the Christian ages from a sensual standard, the church teaching that woman was made for man still exerts its poisonous influence, still destroys women."

The development of ever more efficient methods of subjugating women themselves argued against the idea that God designed it. Evidence that woman's position during the Christian era had undergone important changes and grown progressively more debased supported Gage's assertions that woman's situation under Christianity had deteriorated and done so in gradual stages. The dogma of celibacy was simply a strategy to elevate the priesthood above the laity for the accumulation of wealth and power at the expense of women.

For Gage, no doctrine in the history of the church better illustrated the disaster to woman than that of "the fall dogma" and its role in the witch hunts of the 14th to 17th centuries. Catholic, Protestant, Lutheran, and Calvinist countries all joined in the fun and burned "witches" with hearty enjoyment. The frenzy even infested the new world. She noted:

First: That women were chiefly accused. The victims were mostly aged women

Second: That men believing in woman's inherent wickedness and understanding neither the mental not the physical peculiarities of her being, ascribed all her idiosyncrasies to witchcraft.

Third: That the clergy inculcated the idea that woman was in league with the devil, and that strong intellect, remarkable beauty, or unusual sickness were in themselves proof of this league.

Of all the spot-on analyses she gave to her interpretations of this time period, probably the most riveting for her time, or any time, was her insight into the actual dimensions of the crime. "When for 'witches' we read 'woman' we gain fuller comprehension of the cruelties inflicted . . . upon this portion of humanity." There it was. This was a *crime against women*. Why? There was no doubt for Gage. ". . . as soon as a system of religion was adopted which taught the greater sinfulness of woman . . . the saying arose 'one wizard to 10,000 witches,' and the persecution for witchcraft became chiefly directed against women." Today's historians have caught up to Gage and are refining her insights, but not refuting them. In a recent article, Gage's analysis is cited as revolutionary in the late 19th century, for her assertion that for "witches" we read "women" "Their histories run hand in hand."[19] It would dismay, but not surprise Gage to hear that:

> In the last decade, United Nations officials have reported a rise in women killed for witchcraft across the globe. In India the problem is particularly well-documented, with older women targeted as scapegoats or as a pretext for seizing their lands and goods. In Saudi Arabia, women have been convicted of witchcraft in the courts, and in Ghana they had been exiled to so-called "witch camps." And, in the United States, a Gallup poll found that 21% of people believed in witches.[20]

Other issues included a consideration of the position of wives in Christian lands; the global effect of Christian missionary work on the position of indigenous women wherever missionaries gained ground; the history of male access to and control of women's bodies; and the position of women in Gage's own time. She simply wasn't having any of the usual blather about how Christianity had elevated women. "Woman's increasing freedom within the last hundred years is not due to the church, but to the printing press, to education, to freethought and other forms of advancing civilization. Christendom and its larger influence through the civil law and other institutions sustained by its approval had offered nothing to women, "nor had the church ever been the leader in great reforms. During the anti-slavery conflict, the American Church was known as the 'bulwark of American slavery.' Its course continues the same in every great contest with wrong."

"I expect savage attacks," she wrote to her son after it was published. In fact, many of the reviews were fairly tame. The Chicago *Inter-Ocean* proclaimed it "bad" but the reviewer read only two chapters. *The New York Times* said it was "a book that would appeal to thinkers." Whatever the reviews, Gage was content. "Even if I should slip out my chief life work, my *Woman, Church and State* is done." What did aggravate her was the realization that her name was still indelibly linked in the public mind to Stanton and Anthony. The reviews invariably referred to her as one of the three leaders of the woman suffrage movement. "I hope," she complained to TC, "that no further mention of either Mrs. Stanton or Miss Anthony will be made. I have suffered too much at their hands to wish to advertise them in any way. If *Woman, Church and State* cannot stand on its own merits, let it fall. I have forbidden Kerr [her publisher] to ever mention those women in connection with me ever again. The have stabbed me in reputation and Susan, at least, has stolen in money from me . . . they are traitors . . . Mrs. Stanton especially, I look upon in woman's battle for freedom as I do on Benedict Arnold . . . she is a traitor to what she knows is right."[21]

A year later she had mellowed only slightly towards Stanton and Anthony. In a letter otherwise occupied with news about fixing her house and problems with her publisher she wrote to T.C.:

> There has in many ways been a persistent effort to crush me, especially by Susan B. and even Mrs. Stanton has been guilty of some despicable meanness and falsehoods. But I still live and I hope they will live ten years longer, each of them. Susan is a thief of money and reputation, Mrs. Stanton is of reputation. Mrs. Allen prophesied my future success and their coming around. I saw symptoms from both last fall but I entirely ignored them. I have no further use for either of them although recognizing the great and good work that both have done in many ways.[22]

The most exciting reaction by far to the book came from the Fayetteville, New York, Board of Education. With all the sagacity for which these bodies are known, one of its members, Thomas W. Sheedy, sent a gift copy donated by Gage for the school library to Anthony Comstock, noted crusader against all forms of vice. Comstock sent it back "with word that he would prosecute any school board that put it in their library." The famed rooter-outer of all things with the slightest whiff of naughtiness continued, "The incidents of victims of lust told in this book are such that if I found a person putting that book indiscriminately before the children I would institute a criminal proceeding against them for doing it." Gage was, of course, prepared for just such a review. The woman who had soundly boxed around Rev. Byron Sunderland back in 1852 was in no way intimidated by this latter-day inquisitor. She shot back at him in an interview:

> I look upon him as a man who is mentally and morally unbalanced, not knowing right from wrong, or the facts of history from "tales of lust." Being intellectually weak, Anthony Comstock misrepresents all works upon which he presumes to pass judgment, and is as dangerous to liberty of speech and of the press as were the old inquisitors, whom he somewhat resembles . . . Buddha declared the only sin to be ignorance. If this be true, Anthony Comstock is a great sinner.[23]

Actually, Gage wasn't overly upset by the incident. In fact, she thought it was, "all right splendid for the book. All it now needs is to get into the Papal *Index Expurgetorius.*" She admitted, however, "if I had the money I'd prosecute him for defamation." For all the flap and foolery, *Woman, Church and State* stayed continuously in print until 1917. It has since been reprinted, first the Persephone Press edition that first led me to Gage in 1980 and then again in an anniversary edition by Sky Carrier Press in 1998. It has remained in print to date and has become a staple in women's studies classes.

Gage's last cackles over reaction to her book came only a month before her death. The NAWSA Washington Convention of 1898 celebrated the 50th anniversary of Seneca Falls and Gage was asked to speak. Illness prevented her from going but she sent her last speech to be read to the convention, "Woman's Demand for Freedom, Its Influence on the World." In remarks prefacing the reading of her speech, Anna Howard Shaw lauded Gage "speaking highly of her work and of *Woman, Church and State* "which must have been a <u>bomb</u> in that pious convention! and . . . especially galling to Susan Anthony who was enraged at the admission of a chapter of that name in the *History of Woman Suffrage* and who utterly refused the gift of the book from me when she called at Fleurnoy Street, Chicago in 1897."[24]

Gage's anger towards Stanton was never as deep as it was towards Anthony. Even while calling Stanton a traitor on page two of a letter to her son, by page three she was an "expert on childhood diseases a woman had to care for in raising a family."25 The November, 1895 celebration of Stanton's birthday and the "Pioneer Reception" to follow marked the occasion for Gage's reconciliation with Stanton. They lunched together and Gage spent a day at Stanton's home in Tenafly. Following the publication of *Woman, Church and State* their mutual interest in the church's impact on woman drew them back together and Gage resumed work on several articles for the second volume of Stanton's *Woman's Bible*. Free to compile her research and publish her finding, as well as reestablish a collaborative working arrangement with Stanton, Gage's revelations of 1890 and her break with NWSA made possible this outpouring of her clear vision on the institutions of church and state.

Her work was not complete, however. She was again involved in a test case for voting and recalled the reaction of Fayetteville women to Anthony's trial two decades earlier. Shortly after supporting Anthony during that trial for voting, Gage had organized Fayetteville women to vote. In a letter to Lillie Devereux Blake she wrote:

The fun of the thing was that I had nine women with me in the sitting room of the hotel. I went down first and offered my vote. I was refused one the grounds that I was a married woman. So then I took down two *single* women who supported themselves and owned their own homes. Their votes were also refused. Then I took down one or more war widows. They too, were refused, and so on through the whole nine. With each one offered I made an appropriate argument and had a big and attentive crowd to hear me. The very worst feature of our case was that it was a corporation tax election; only taxpayers were called on to vote on the raising of money for putting in waterworks, etc. The largest taxpayer in the village was a woman, as was the smallest. The women I offered were all taxpayers, and even I was a taxpayer, in addition to my husband's being one. It caused a great stir.26

Twenty years later she was arrested for registering to vote for the School Commissioner election. She had not actually registered herself, although she had intended to. Someone else had submitted her name which she discovered on the evening of October 21, 1893, when

"Deputy Sheriff Bennett of Syracuse served a Supreme Writ upon me to appear before Judge M. Lemmon" the following "Monday morning at 10 o'clock." Because this was a test case to decide the eligibility of women to vote for this office, her lawyer advised her that he wanted women willing to try to vote so he could bring a case against the inspectors also. "Therefore, I marshalled several women to each polling booth were we were refused as I had expected." She lost and lost again on appeal in the decision, characterized as an "unintentional satire" of a legal decision in the fourth volume of the *History* filling many pages with its "hairsplitting definitions." It claimed that, "although women could vote for school officers, that was due to there having originally been appointive positions, the legislature then making them elective, but the school Commissioner was an elective office under the state constitution and women were forbidden to vote under the constitution." Anthony wrote inquiring about the case, but Gage was not moved. "Susan" she noted, "[was] quick to see anything to her advantage." Two years more passed before Gage could be anything more than polite where Anthony was concerned.[27]

The years between her break with Anthony and NWSA and her death were by any measure some of her most productive in a life noted for its productivity. Matilda Joslyn Gage died on March 18, 1898, at the age of seventy-two at her daughter Maud's home in Chicago. Although much younger than Stanton and Anthony she was often mistaken for the oldest of the three. A poem written to celebrate the suffrage leaders included this verse:

And with our reverence for age
First comes Matilda Joslyn Gage.

Poor health had plagued her off and on all her life but her letters during the last six months of her life attest to a more pronounced concern with doctors as well as home remedies. In September, 1897, she advised T.C. that she had "been suffering indigestion and am using cayenne pepper on my food. Mrs. Dr. Lozier recommended it." November found her frustrated, "I could have done more, been more to myself and the world had I always been of the strong health of Mrs. Stanton and Miss

Anthony." By January she had turned to more radical measures, "I have been drinking beer and am now using six-year old port."

Her one important disappointment during this time was that she was too ill to deliver her own speech at the Fiftieth Anniversary Convention in Washington, "I did so hope to go to the Fiftieth . . . but, of course, had to give that up." Her last letter to her son, however, shows her spirited approach to life's troubles lasted until the end. "Now, on sale of building and lot, altho' I should prefer not to sell for a saloon, yet I would sell to one, rather than not sell and suffer as we do for means to use to live."[28]

She was a revolutionary. She was well ahead of her time. As Dr. Stuard concludes in her analysis of *Woman*, "She aspired to become a rigorous, documented-based scholar of history and one who aspired to a global perspective on the past." And, "that given the limitations of her reading matter, her history still stands as inspired for its insights and daring. That she left her readers dismayed by her conclusions should not blind us to the excellence of her work as an historian."[29]

In complete keeping with the causes and concerns of her life, she was cremated, according to her wishes, because it was "the quickest, the most cleanly method and the purest for the earth." Her ashes were returned to Fayetteville, where she was buried.

NOTES

1. "The Loss of Woman Suffrage in South Dakota," *The Woman's Tribune*, Dec. 4, 1890, 194.
2. MJG to Thomas Clarkson Gage, March 4, 1890.
3. MJG, "The Dangers of the Hour," Woman's National Liberal Union Convention, 1890, reprinted in Kohrs Campbell, Karlyn, *Man Cannot Speak For Her, Key Texts at the Early Feminists*, 340-370.
4. *Ibid.*, 348.
5. Susan Mosher Stuard (2017) Matilda Gage Writes a World History of Women, *Women's History Review*, 26:6, 900-914, DOI: 10.1080/09612015.2016.1228282
6. *Ibid.*
7. MJG to TCG, Nov. 15, 1897.
8. MJG to TCG, Jan. 21, 1872 and Aug. 31, 1882; *HWS*, IV, 28-30.
9. William Leach, *True Love and Perfect Union*, (New York: Basic Books, 1980) 278.
10. Gage, Matilda Joslyn, *WCS*, (Watertown, Mass.: Persephone Press, 1980) 5 and 241-2.

11. Gage's themes were still current in the late 1960s and 1970s when a trickle of work on women's history began. Gage's chapter on "The Matriarchate" is echoed in Elaine Pagel's, "What Became of God the Mother? Conflicting Images of God in Early Christianity" (1976), Julia O'Faolain and Lauro Martines's, *Not in God's Image, (1973)*, Merlin Stone's, *When God Was a Woman*, (1976), Sarah B. Pomeroy's, *Goddesses, Whores, Wives, and Slaves: Women in Classical Antiquity*, (1975), Carol Christ's, *Diving Deep and Surfacing*, (1980) and many others. This particular area of research has yielded so much interest in women's place in the "old religions" that "Goddess Tours" to Crete with Carol Christ were regularly advertised in *The Now Times* and *The Women's Review of Books*. As of this writing Goddess Tours are offered by at least three tour companies.
https://www.goddessariadne.org/
https://herpathoflove.com/workshops-tours/atlantis-goddess-pilgrimage-greece/
and https://www.womentravel.info/profile.php?id=577
This last continues to feature the expertise of Carol Christ.
Other themes such as women's work, the beauty trap, divorce, custody, and property laws, comparable pay and pay for domestic labor, and the abuse of women are important topics throughout the literature of Women's Studies as well as the daily newspapers.

12. ECS, *Woman's Bible*, 8.

13. MJG to TCG, Dec. 2, 1886.

14. MJG to TCG, Aug. 11, 1884 and Stearns, Bertha-Monica, "Reform Periodicals and Female Reformers," *The American Historical Review*, XXXVII, Oct., 1931-July, 1932, 689-92.

15. Bass, Dorothy C., "Their Prodigious Influence, Women, Religion and Reform in Antebellum America," 286-7 in Ruether, Rosemary and Eleanor McLaughlin, eds., *Women of Spirit, Female Leadership in the Jewish and Christian Traditions*, (New York: Simon & Schuster) 1979. 297. And MJG to TCG, Jan. 11, 1888 and Feb. 3, 1888.

16. Post, Albert, *Popular Freethought in America*, (New York: Columbia Univ. Press, 1943, reprinted. Octagon Books, 1974, 30-31, 226, &

17. ECS, *Woman's Bible*, 12-13

18. All quotes are from *WC&S*, Chapter One.

19. Demos, John Putnam, *Entertaining Satan, Witchcraft and the Culture of Early New England*, (Oxford University Press) updated edition 2004. Reis, Elizabeth, *Damned Women, Sinners and Witches in Puritan New England*, (New York: Cornell University Press) 1997 and Corey, Mary E., "Matilda Joslyn Gage: A Nineteenth-Century Women's Rights Historian Looks at Witchcraft," in The Organization of American Historians *Magazine of History*, Special Issue: Witchcraft, Vol 17, No. 4, July 2003. Madeline Miller, "From Circe to Clinton: why powerful women are cast as witches," *The Guardian*, Sat. 7, 2018.

20. Miller, 6.

21. MJG to TCG, Feb., 1893. In another letter to TCG, July 11, 1893, that mentions the theft of money refers to Gage's dissatisfaction with the terms regarding Anthony's buyout of her interest in the *HWS*. Another damaged letter from MJG to TCG dated June, 1885 reads: Mrs. Stanton threatens to [illegible]

Miss Anthony if she does not pay her something. Miss A. strives in every way to compel [illegible] work for nothing [illegible] <u>charge</u> to *HWS* expenses money spent in the Nebraska and Oregon campaigns and part of the Washington convention expenses of last winter, also other equally ridiculous things such as claiming for *Revolution* work $10,000 when I heard from her own lips that over one half was given her in large sums <u>without interest</u> from $2,000-$4,000 besides the smaller sums. By the contract she [illegible] to make mis[leading? or [mis] statements to Mrs. Stanton and myself. It is nine and [one?] half years since that contract was signed and <u>yesterday</u> was the first anything like a statement was ever received from her and that was [illegible] a most [illegible] document and most outrageous in its dishonesty. But all this is private for the present.

22. MJG to TCG July 14, 1894
23. *Ibid.*, August 3, 1894 and Wagner, 247.
24. MJG fragment, February, 24, 1898 and notation on the back of her speech. The address is the home of her daughter, Maud and her husband, L. F. Baum.
25. MJG to TCG, July 11, 1893.
26. Blake, *Champion of Women*, p. 108 and *HWS*, IV, 868.
27. MJG to TCG, Nov. 7, 1893; Nov. 22, 1897; Sept. 22, 1897, Nov. 15, 1897 and MJG to Helen Leslie Gage, Jan. 15, 1898.
28. MJG to Helen Leslie Gage, Sept, 9, 1897 and MJG to TCG, March 9, 1898.
29. Stuard, 910.

CHAPTER 6

The End? Not Yet!

. . . they, not ourselves, shall enter into the harvest

HOW do you summarize the larger than life contributions of someone who, in her lifetime, worked tirelessly in the shadow of two giants without sounding as though you're overstating her worth? We can start by digging beneath the surface glow to find the real substance and sum of her career. Rather than relying on the often-self-aggrandizing estimations written by these two giants, Stanton and Anthony, and their admirers, we need to sort through the records and do our own evaluations. Scrolling through miles of microfilm yielded an exciting trove of material about, by, and to Gage. That this trove came directly from the Stanton-Anthony Papers[1] is in itself a clear rebuttal of the short shrift they each gave to Gage in their memoirs and autobiographies. The Matilda Joslyn Gage Papers are still on microfilm and available in most academic libraries.[2] The *National Citizen and Ballot Box* is available through academic libraries in digital form or by individual subscription.[3]

The legacy of Gage's life can be found in the causes she espoused, the events she lived and chronicled, and the history she wrote. While Stanton and Anthony have been thrown the lion's share of bouquets, women like Gage, especially Gage, were doing the yeoman-like work of the movement – really making it move. Was she snarky at times? Well, yes. But weren't they all? And would you expect less from folks working in close quarters for half a century.

Philosophically of one mind with Stanton, she was a well-matched collaborator. With Anthony she willingly dove into the work of NWSA performing all the quotidian tasks organizations require. As the Chair of the Executive Committee for most of her forty-year tenure with NWSA, she left her mark on its decisions, petitions, resolutions, declarations, and conventions. In this position, she also provided the "meat and potatoes" of NWSA paperwork; correspondences, invitations, regrets and acceptances, schedules, speeches, and more. As a writer during her affiliation with NWSA she published its newspaper, *National Citizen and Ballot Box* and, as has been demonstrated in Chapter Three, wrote more than half of the material in the *HWS*, Volumes I-III.[4] Whereas Anthony was the complete, administrator, organizer, and activist, and Stanton the acknowledged philosopher, Gage complemented them both. She was committed to the work of the organization and could hold her own philosophically and intellectually with Stanton. It is easy to see why in their day they were called "the triumvirate."

To say it was difficult for Gage to leave the NWSA would be an understatement of monumental proportions. She had given her life and energy to it for over forty years. Small comfort that she was only the first of a series of what Ellen Carol DuBois identified as "the organizational secessions that plagued NAWSA."[5] Actually these secessions might be better characterized as expulsions, in view of the active efforts by Anthony and her "nieces" to marginalize women considered to be too radical or too partisan. For her efforts to prevent NWSA from uniting with AWSA, attempting as she did a direct challenge to Anthony's power, she became the first of many long-standing leaders set aside by the new generation of suffrage ladies. I use the term ladies purposefully. The time of acting on behalf of women had been eroding over the course of the last decade of the 19th century. Anthony's courting of Frances Willard and her WCTU, her elevating of what Stanton called "society women" to leadership positions they soon demonstrated they were in no way capable of occupying, and the "late-night, eleventh hour" agreement to the merger were all ominous signs that Anthony had emerged as the sole face of woman suffrage. She and the ladies were now completely in charge. No wonder the organization drifted for the next two decades.

The events surrounding the merger and the years Anthony led the association without the counsel of Stanton and Gage suggest a reappraisal of Anthony's leadership. Anthony, indeed, not these women, singly or together, could have prevented the trend toward conservatism within the movement – it tends to happen in all organizations that start out on the cutting edge. And, they were in no position powerful enough to buck the increasingly conservative political scene at the end of the century. But, Anthony and her girls embraced it. Her single-minded push for woman suffrage can be seen as admirable – political movements need people willing to steadfastly pursue a goal. On the other hand, as all manner of women's rights issues fell to the wayside, what was left of an agenda for using the vote once achieved?

Gage's decision to leave NWSA, however painful, resulted in the time she needed to organize twenty and more years of investigating woman's role in society and publish her *Woman, Church and State.* The conservative bent that had forced her to leave NWSA made publishing her finding more urgent. She wrote in the preface, 'This work explains itself and is given to the world because it is needed." She then dedicated it "to all Persons, who breaking away from custom and the usage of ages, dare speak Truth for the sake of Truth. To all such it will be welcome; to all others aggressive and educational."[6]

Her analysis of woman's position over time *vis à vis* church and state demonstrated that "whenever we find laws of the state bearing with greater hardship upon woman than upon man, we shall ever find them due to the teachings of the church." Most of the "history" written by suffrage women was laudatory or cautionary. Gage's offered more. Her evidence of changes in woman's position over time showed that woman had not occupied a static, "God given" position, but had felt the impact of a lowering of status as the "priestly class" interpreted scripture in their own self interest and accumulated power at woman's expense. Her thesis was that church dogma blaming woman for "the fall" was integral to its teachings, not incidental, and, therefore, explains woman's inferior position in the church. Without a "fall" there would be no need for a savior. Woman was to blame for the loss of Eden! At the heart of her thesis was the concept of change. The fact that woman's position had undergone change and was not identical in all times and places, offered the opportunity for women to make change happen. Change argued against the idea that woman's position was fixed. Her analysis of this change opened up worlds of possibility.

The danger in her day was the profusion of Christian churches and associations determined to undermine the liberal principles of republican government with Sunday observance (blue) laws, with the abolition of civil marriage ceremonies, with federal laws restricting divorce and with a proposed constitutional amendment changing the preamble to recognize "Almighty God as the source of all power and authority in civil government, . . . and the Bible as the standard to decide all moral issues in political life. The chief danger of the present situation lies in the fact that the majority of the people do not see that there is danger.[7]

Gage's thoughts on the importance of the suffrage movement and women's history were always expressed as a confident hope that the future would be better for "those who would come after." No one's future concerned her more than that of her four children and their children.

Helen Leslie, named for her grandmother, was born November 3, 1845. Thomas Clarkson, to whom the bulk of Gage's correspondence was addressed, arrived on July 19, 1848. Her second son, Charles Henry, died soon after his birth in January, 1850. Julia Louise was born on May 21, 1851. Her youngest, Maud, was born March 27, 1861. By the time Gage plunged into National suffrage work in 1869, Helen was twenty-four and living at home, T.C. was twenty-one and a student at Cornell. Julia was eighteen and also living at home. This made it possible for Gage to leave her youngest, eight-year-old Maud at home in her sisters' care during her speaking tours and conventions. Letters home brought details of the suffrage work and the excitement of Washington to Fayetteville. She also arranged to take one or more of her kids with her whenever possible. In fact, she and her daughter Helen attended their first suffrage convention together in 1852 when Helen was only six.

As Gage's schedule became busier, her husband seemed to take it all in stride. In a series of letters to T.C. at Cornell, the first written on May 14, 1871, he writes, "Your mother is expected tomorrow." On May 19, he guesses, ". . . she must have gone to Vineland [New Jersey].

May 20, he can report, "Your mother has gone to Chicago. She wrote from Vineland last Saturday night. I expect she will be home in about two weeks more."[8]

"Clarky, I want you to bring my revolver and cartridges!" she ordered her son. During the June preparations for the Centennial celebration in Philadelphia, emotions ran "wild" over opening the exhibition on Sundays. Anthony and Gage attended a "great meeting favoring it" and "now I want my revolver."[9] All four children joined her in Philadelphia but there is no record of whether or not T.C. brought her revolver!

Gage was a good mother, always concerned about her children – sometimes maybe a little overly so. When Helen was unmarried and depressed about it at thirty-one, Gage agonized over what to do, confiding to T.C. that she wished Helen would "find a business or marry but get out of Fayetteville!" When Helen did marry, she worried, "He is an old man and I fear her future is not very bright." Julia married Frank Carpenter who turned out to be unsuccessful, alcoholic, and abusive. Gage wanted her and the babies to come home to Fayetteville but knew "Care must be used so as not to have that hound, out of spite, keep the children . . . I am bitterly opposed to a woman yielding her person to a drunkard. It is most dreadful." T.C.'s marriage was happier. After a short stint working in his father's dry goods store, he went into partnership with the Beard brothers, Frank and Charles. They followed opportunity in the west and moved to the Dakota Territory and opened a store. There he met and married Sophie T. Jewell. Gage sent her best wishes and "enclosed a spray of lilies of the valley" hoping their "married life as sweet, lovely and pure as these delicate flowers." Because she could not travel to his wedding, "she, Helen & Charley & Leslie (their daughter) celebrated 'a wedding' with cake, ice cream and candles lit." Although she was delighted with T.C.'s happiness, when she heard from a friend in England about the possibility of "spirit husbands in the next life" she thought "If there are such marriages in the next world as she claims, I am going to stick here as long as I can and escape them."[10]

Her home in Fayetteville was rarely empty, even after her children were married. Helen and Charley and their daughter, Leslie, lived with

Gage for several years before joining T.C. in South Dakota. Maud and her husband, L. Frank Baum were regular company during the lean years before his writing became profitable and they moved to Chicago. Julia finally came home with her children, Harry and Magdalena. But when they were away, some of her most charming letters were sent to her grandkids. To them she announced the first snowdrops in her garden, described the Fayetteville fireworks on the Fourth, and explained how to decorate with autumn leaves. She wanted to know if they were learning to sew and sent them patterns for dresses in the latest styles. She sent recipes and mittens, and always a book. It may seem odd to us today, but all of the suffragists were acutely aware of the value of their work, that they were making history as well as chronicling it. So, sending bound volumes of the *National Citizen and Ballot Box* and the *History of Woman Suffrage* to them was completely sensible. Don't forget Gage's controlling thesis throughout all of her work was the need to recover and never again lose women's past. Preserving and sending forward the works of her lifetime to her grandchildren was completely in keeping with that.

Gage was a complicated woman. As a scholar she was relentless in her search for the truth about women's lives and fearless in her condemnation of the systematic degradation inflicted on them by both church and state. As our first *bona fide* woman's historian, she advocated in every forum open to her for education for women; the only way forward was for women to know their collective past. She was no less committed to keeping the ideals that she was fighting for at the top of the suffrage agenda and at the heart of the organization to which she gave her life.

The stormy merger of NWSA and AWSA in 1890 stirred many NWSA leaders to challenge Anthony's machinations to effect the merger on behalf of the entire NWSA and to protest what the merger would mean for NWSA's delegate structure, as well as the ominous and imminent elevation of conservatives to positions of leadership. Gage led the opposition to Anthony's decision. When it became clear that the merger couldn't be stopped, she left rather than to participate in what soon became a shadow of the old NWSA. It is in the battles fought over the merger that the clearest view of the changed nature of the relationships among the NWSA leaders can be seen and Anthony's singular authority becomes most starkly evident.

If Gage had done nothing further after leaving NWSA, her career as an activist, writer, and historian would be important enough to warrant study. But, her years after NWSA were some of her most productive. She and Stanton reconciled their differences and collaborated once more on a writing project that became *The Woman's Bible*. Her most important work, though, was *Woman, Church and State*. The "church diggings" that Anthony had so often ridiculed was organized and published in 1893. It can surely be called the first volume of women's history and was the only monograph to emerge from the 19th-century woman suffrage movement. It expanded freethought doctrine by arguing from a feminist perspective and offered a critical analysis of the history of women under Christianity. Meeting the church on its own terms she debunked its proclamations that asserted that women's position under Christianity was superior to her position in any other time and place. In arguments as relevant today as they were then, she arrayed her evidence to the contrary. By doing so she transcended the limited reform agenda of "woman suffrage" to leave a roadmap to the future for all women.

As an historian Gage was acutely aware that the past could unlock the door to the future. She predicted, "A brighter day is to come for the world, a day when the intuitions of woman's soul shall be accepted as part of humanity's spiritual wealth; when force shall step backward, and love, in reality, rule the teachings of religion; and may woman be strong in the ability and courage necessary to bring about this millennial time."[11]

NOTES

1. They have since been digitalized and can be found at http://ecssba.rutgers.edu/index.html "To the editors, Patricia G. Holland and Ann D. Gordon, should go the thanks and support of every woman in America." Lynne Sherr
2. The Matilda Joslyn Gage Papers: http://oasis.lib.harvard.edu/oasis/deliver/~sch00214
3. *National Citizen and Ballot Box:* http://www.accessible-archives.com/collections/national-citizen-and-ballot-box/
4. To this writer, volumes I-III are the only volumes worth reading. The others under the direction of Anthony and written with the leaden pen of Ida Husted Harper are soporific.

5. DuBois, Ellen Carol, ed., *Elizabeth Cady Stanton, Susan B. Anthony Correspondence, Writings, Speeches,* (New York: Schocken Books, 1981) 181.

6. *WCS,* 3 & 5.

7. Gage, "The Dangers of the Hour," Women's National Liberal convention, 1890, in Kohrs Campbell, 363.

8. Henry H. Gage to TCG May 14, 17, 19, and 20, 1871.

9. MJG to TCG, July ?, 1876.

10. *Ibid.,* June, 1885.

11. *WC&S,* 245.

Acknowledgements

WRITING is a lonely pursuit. It's you, your computer, your cup of cold coffee, and the blank screen and pulsing cursor in front of you. If it's a history, though, you have companions. On the floor and scattered around the workroom are stacks of articles, reels of microfilm, print outs, reference books, and yellow pads of notes that represent the work of the scholars who've come before you. Of primary importance for this work, was and continues to be the historians who created and brought legitimacy to the field of women's studies when many saw it as unimportant at best and frivolous at worst. So, to them I give a full measure of gratitude.

For me, three scholars stand out as beacons along the way. First is my graduate advisor, Mary Young, Professor of History Emerita at the University of Rochester, who saw value in exploring the work of Matilda Joslyn Gage and offered steady encouragement in spite of the prevailing reservations within scholarly circles about women's history as suitably weighty. Second is Susan Mosher Stuard, Professor of History Emerita at Haverford College. It was in her undergraduate class on women in the middle ages, that I first encountered Gage while doing research into the centuries referred to as "the burning time" of the European witch hunts. Gage's name resurfaced in graduate school, now in the context of the woman suffrage movement. I remember meeting Prof. Stuard at the Berkshire Conference on the History of Women when I was quite frustrated with my research and ready to give it up. "We need your research!" she said, "you need to keep working." And, so I did. Third, is Sally Roesch Wagner, Executive Director of the Gage Foundation. I first met Prof. Wagner by way of her Introduction to the Persephone Press reprint of Gage's, *Woman, Church, and State.* Her introduction so piqued my curiosity about Gage, I determined to make her life's work, mine. Since then, I've come to know her as a colleague and have always appreciated her support of my work. I stand in awe of her dedication to the Gage Foundation. My work stands on the shoulders of great scholars.

Regarding the actual work, I want to thank the following:

Many thanks go to my colleagues who agreed to review drafts of the manuscript. This is a time-consuming but necessary task that we do for each other, but for scholars busy with their own research as well as hectic teaching schedules, it's a lot to ask. To these stalwarts, Diane Fulkerson, Director of Information Commons at the University of South Florida Sarasota-Manatee, Tricia Stewart, Associate Professor, Western Connecticut State University, Kate Estey Kramer, College Board Faculty Consultant for Advanced Placement, U. S. History and Program Developer and Coordinator for Federal Teaching American History Grants for South Dakota K-12 Teachers, and Sally Roesch Wagner, Executive Director of the Gage Foundation, I am forever in their debt. The work is much stronger because of their comments, corrections, and suggestions. Any errors, and a few typos probably did slip though, are, however, mine and mine alone.

Many thanks to Anne Kilgore, Head Bazoo at Paperwork, my editor, book designer, cheerleader, friend, guide, and sister who worked with me from the start. This is our third publishing adventure together and I have come to depend on her infinite patience, her amazing creativity, and expert guidance. Likewise, I want to thank my publisher, James Madden, at Paramount Books. He's never hesitated to offer me all his expertise and experience as a publisher as well as the resources to move my work from manuscript to print.

In the interests of full disclosure, I have to admit that the bulk of the research for this book was completed by 2000. Then, like the *History of Woman Suffrage* project itself, life intruded and other projects interrupted the work. But, as you will see, one of the driving forces that brought the

Stanton, Anthony, Gage volumes of the *HWS* to completion was Gage, herself. She was a dynamo and despite her frequent protestations of feeling poorly, she was one of the prime movers that made the suffrage movement move. Since 2000, she has sat on her appointed shelf in my office where her ghostly disgruntled harrumph would greet me every day. She's an awful nag but her presence finally pushed and prodded me to update, add to, and complete the project; to get the part of her story that I was privy to out into the world. Now that it's done, I must say, it's rather nice to be able to walk into my office and not hear her grumbling. So, lastly, I want to thank Matilda Joslyn Gage for her life's work that, in many ways, made my life's work possible.

For Book Club Discussions

1. In the first two chapters, the author gives the reader a bit of her own background to set the stage. In what ways did that add to or detract from the reader's interest in Gage?

2. As all politics is local, all history is local, too. What elements of the upstate New York location would you say were significant to the launch of the women's rights movement?

3. If you had the chance to talk with the author, what questions would you want to ask about her research?

4. Even today, women's rights are still questioned, even women voting has its detractors. What do you think kept these women of the 19th century persisting in the face of overwhelming opposition?

5. If you could go back in time and join their struggle, what would you contribute to the movement?

6. As you read in the last chapter, two new paths for studying Gage have opened recently. One path focuses on her research into the burning time of witch hunts in Europe during the middle ages. The second focuses on her research as a pioneer in the world history movement. In what ways, if any, do you think these new scholarly trends will affect her legacy?

7. Initially, woman suffrage was only one of the elements of the women's rights movement but by the end of the 19th century it became the singular goal. What was won for women and what was lost to women as a result of this narrowing of focus?

8. Do you see any connections between the working lives of Stanton, Gage, and Anthony and your own?

References

Works Cited

Anthony, Susan B. and Ida Husted Harper, *History of Woman Suffrage*, IV, Indianapolis: Hollenbeck Press, 1902.

The Ballot Box, Toledo, Ohio.

Banner, Lois, *Elizabeth Cady Stanton: A Radical for Women's Rights*, Boston: Little, Brown, 1980.

Barry, Kathleen, *Susan B. Anthony, A Biography*, New York: New York University Press, 1988.

Behnke, Donna, *Religious Issues in Nineteenth Century Feminism*, Troy, N.Y.: Whitston Publishing, 1982.

Blackwell, Alice Stone, *Lucy Stone: Pioneer for Women's Rights*, Boston: Little, Brown, 1930.

Blake, Katherine Devereux and Mary Louise Wallace, *Champion of Women: The Life of Lillie Devereux Blake*, New York: Fleming H. Revell Co., 1943.

Brammer, Leila R., *Excluded From Suffrage History: Matilda Joslyn Gage, Nineteenth Century American Feminist*, Westport, Conn: Greenwood Press, 2000.

Bruce, Dwight H., *Onondaga's Centennial, Gleanings of a Century*, I & II, Boston: Boston History Company Publishers, 1896.

Buhle, Mari Jo and Paul Buhle, Eds. *The Concise History of Woman Suffrage*, Chicago: University of Illinois Press, 1978.

Cole, Charlotte, *Olympia Brown: The Battle for Equality*, Racine, WI, Mother Courage Press, 1988.

DuBois, Ellen Carol, Ed., *Elizabeth Cady Stanton/Susan B. Anthony Correspondence, Writings, Speeches*, New York: Schocken Books, 1981.

_____, *Feminism and Suffrage, The Emergence of an Independent Woman's Movement in America 1848-1869*, Ithaca, N.Y.: Cornell University Press, 1978.

_____, "Introduction," *Feminist Theorists, Three Centuries of Key Women Thinkers*, Ed., Dale Spender, New York: Pantheon Books, 1983.

_____, "On Labor and Free Love: Two Unpublished Speeches of Elizabeth Cady Stanton," *Signs: Journal of Women in Culture and Society*, Vol. 1, No. 1, 1975.

_____, "The Radicalism of the Woman Suffrage Movement: Notes Toward the Reconstruction of Nineteenth-century Feminism, *Feminist Studies*, Vol. 3, Fall, 1975.

_____, "Working Women, Class Relations and Suffrage Militance: Harriot Stanton Blatch and the New York Woman Suffrage Movement," *Journal of American History*, Vol. 74, No. 1 June, 1987.

_____, "Outgrowing the Compact of the Fathers, Equal Rights, Woman Suffrage and the United States Constitution, 1820-1878," *Journal of American History*, Vol. 74, No. 3, December, 1987.

Duniway, Abigail Scott, *Pathbreaking, An Autobiographical History of the Equal Suffrage Movement in Pacific Coast States*, 2nd. Ed., 1914, New York: Kraus, (reprint) 1971.

Edwards, G. Thomas, *Sowing Good Seeds, The Northwest Suffrage Campaigns of Susan B. Anthony*, Portland, Oregon: Historical Society Press, 1990.

Fayetteville Gazette, Fayetteville, New York, 1862.

Fayetteville Recorder, Fayetteville, New York, 1848-1898.

Fenton, Zanita E., "No Witch is a Bad Witch: A Commentary on the Erasure of Matilda Joslyn Gage," *Southern California Interdisciplinary Law Journal*, Vol. 20, 2010.

Freedman, Estelle, "Separation as Strategy: Female Institution

Building and American Feminism, 1870-1930," *Feminist Studies,* Vol. 5, No. 3, Fall, 1979.

Flexner, Eleanor, *Century of Struggle,* rev. ed., Cambridge: Harvard University Press, 1975.

Foner, Philip S., *The Life and Major Writings of Thomas Paine,* New York: Carol Publishing Group, 1993.

Gage, Matilda Joslyn, "Arguments Before the Committee on the District of Columbia, 1876.

_____, *National Citizen and Ballot Box,* Syracuse, 1878-1881.

_____, "Speech at Woman's Rights Convention," Syracuse, New York, 1852.

_____, "Who Planned the Tennessee Campaign"

_____, "Woman as Inventor"

_____, *Woman, Church and State,* reprint edition, 1980, Watertown, Massachusetts: Persephone Press from 1893 edition in its entirety, Introduction by Sally Roesch Wagner and Forward by Mary Daly.

_____, "Woman's Rights Catechism," *Weekly Recorder,* Fayetteville, New York, July 27, 1871.

Gardner, Martin and Russell B. Nye, *The Wizard of Oz and Who He Was,* East Lansing: Michigan State University Press, 1957.

Gill, Katherine, "Why Women Have No Useable Past," *New York Times Book Review,* May 2, 1993.

Griffith, Elisabeth, *In Her Own Right: The Life of Elizabeth Cady Stanton,* New York: Oxford University Press, 1985.

Gurko, Miriam, *The Ladies of Seneca Falls,* New York: Macmillan Publishers, 1974.

Hall, Florence Howe, *Julia Ward Howe and the Woman Suffrage Movement,* New York: Arno Press (reprint) 1969.

Hanaford, Phebe A., *Daughters of America or Woman of the Century,* Augusta, Maine: True and Company, 1882.

Harper, Ida Husted, *The Life and Work of Susan B. Anthony,* I-III, Indianapolis and Kansas City: Bowen-Merrill Company, 1898.

Hays, Elinor Rice, *Morning Star, A Biography of Lucy Stone 1818-1893,* New York: Harcourt, Brace & World, 1961.

James, Edward T., et al., eds. *Notable American Women 1607-1950: A Biographical Dictionary,* I & II, Cambridge: Harvard University Press, 1971.

Kephart, John Edgar, *A Voice for Freedom: The Signal of Liberty 1841-1848,* diss, University of Michigan, 1960.

Kern, Kathi, *Mrs. Stanton's Bible,* Ithaca: Cornell University Press, 2001,

Kerr, Andrea Moore, *Lucy Stone, Speaking Out for Equality,* New Brunswick, N.J.: Scarecrow Press, 1972.

Kohrs Campbell, Karlyn, "Stanton's 'The Solitude of Self': A Rationale for Feminism," *Quarterly Journal of Speech,* Vol. 66, 1980.

_____, *Man Cannot Speak For Her, Key Texts of the Early Feminists,* I & II, New York: Greenwood Press, 1989.

Kraditor, Aileen S., *The Ideas of the Woman Suffrage Movement, 1890-1920,* New York: Columbia University Press, 1965.

Leach, William, *True Love and Perfect Union, The Feminist Reform of Sex and Society,* New York: Basic Books, 1980.

Lutz, Alma, *Created Equal, A Biography of Elizabeth Cady Stanton 1815-1902,* New York: Farrar, Straus and Giroux, 1974.

Martin, Wendy, ed., *The American Sisterhood of the Feminist Movement from Colonial Times to the Present,* New York: Harper & Row, 1972.

Masel-Waters, Lynne, "Their Rights and Nothing More: A History of *The Revolution, 1868-70," Journalism Quarterly,* Vol. 53, Summer, 1976.

Mather, Anne, "A History of Feminist Periodicals, Parts I & II, *Journalism History,* Vol. 1, Spring, 1974.

McDonald, David Kevin, *Organizing Womanhood: Women's Culture and the Politics of Woman Suffrage in New York State 1865-1917,* unpublished diss., State University of New York at Stony Brook, 1971.

Miller, Madeline, "From Circe to Clinton: why powerful women are cast as witches," *The Guardian,* April 7, 2018.

Mott, Frank Luther, *American Journalism: A History of Newspapers Through 250 Years, 1690-1940*, New York: Macmillan Publishers, 1941.

National Citizen and Ballot Box, Syracuse, N. Y., 1878-1881.

O'Neill, William, *Everyone Was Brave: The Rise and Fall of Feminism in America*, Quadrangle Books, 1970.

Parkman, Francis, "The Failure of Universal Suffrage," *North American Review*, No. CCLXIII, July-August, 1878.

Post, Albert, *Popular Freethought in America, 1825-1850*, New York: Columbia University Press, 1943, reprint Octagon Books, 1974.

Rakow, Lana and Cheris Kramarae, eds., *The Revolution in Words, Righting Women, 1868-1871*, New York: Routledge Press, 1990, revised ed., 2010.

Reis, Elizabeth, ed. Organization of American Historians, *Magazine of History*, Vol. 17, No. 4, July, 2003, Special Issue on Witchcraft.

The Revolution, 1868-1870.

Rich, Adrienne, *A Wild Patience Has Taken Me This Far, Poems 1978-1981*, New York: W.W. Norton, 1981.

Rossi, Alice S., ed., *The Feminist Papers from Adams to de Beauvoir*, New York: Bantam Books, 1973.

Ruether, Rosemary and Eleanor McLaughlin, eds., *Women of Spirit, Female Leadership in the Jewish and Christian Traditions*, New York: Simon & Schuster, 1979.

Schaffer, Ronald, "The Problem of Consciousness in the Woman Suffrage Movement: A California Perspective," *Pacific Historical Review*, Vol. 45, Nov., 1976.

Scott, Anne Firor and Scott, Andrew MacKay, *One Half the People/ The Fight for Woman Suffrage*, Urbana, Chicago: University of Illinois Press, 1982.

Solomon, Martha M., ed., *A Voice of Their Own: The Woman Suffrage Press*, Tuscaloosa: University of Alabama Press, 1991.

Spender, Dale, ed., *Feminist Theorists/Three Centuries of Key Women Thinkers*, New York: Random House, 1983.

_____, *Women of Ideas and What Men Have Done to Them from Aphra Behn to Adrienne Rich*, London, Boston: Routledge & Kegan Paul, 1982.

Stanton, Elizabeth Cady, *Eighty Years and More/Reminiscences 1815-1897*, reprint from the T. Fisher Unwin edition of 1898, New York: Schocken Books, 1971.

_____, Susan B. Anthony, Matilda Joslyn Gage, *History of Woman Suffrage*, I-III, New York: Fowler & Wells, 1881, 1882, 1886.

_____, and Revising Committee, *The Woman's Bible, Parts I and II*, New York: Arno Press 1972, reprint from 1895 and 1898 editions.

Stanton, Theodore and Harriott Stanton Blatch, eds. *Elizabeth Cady Stanton as Revealed in Her Letters, Diary, and Reminiscences*, Vol. I & II, New York: Harper & Brothers, 1922.

Stearns, Bertha Monica, "Reform Periodicals and Female Reformers, 1830-1860," *American Historical Review*, Vol. 37, 1932.

Strom, Sharon Hartman, "leadership and Tactics in the American Woman Suffrage Movement: A New Perspective from Massachusetts," *Journal of American History*, Vol. 62, No. 2, Sept., 1975.

Stuard, Susan Mosher, "Matilda Gage Writes a World History of Women," *Woman's History Review*, Vol. 26, No. 6, 2017.

Taylor, Barbara, *Eve and the New Jerusalem, Social Feminism in the Nineteenth Century*, New York: Pantheon Books, 1983.

Tetrault, Lisa, *The Myth of Seneca Falls: Memory and the Women's Suffrage Movement, 1848-1898*. Gender and American Culture Series, Chapel Hill: University of North Carolina Press, 2014.

Waggen-Spack, Beth M., *The Search for Self-Sovereignty: The Oratory of Elizabeth Cady Stanton*, New York: Greenwood Press, 1989.

Wagner, Sally Roesch, *A Time of Protest, Suffragists Challenge the Republic: 1870-1887*, Sacramento: Spectrum Publications, 1987.

_____, "New Women's History Videos," Review in *NWSA Journal*, Vol. 12, No. 2, Summer, 2000.

Welter, Barbara, "The Cult of True Womanhood: 1820-1860," *American Quarterly*, Vol. 18, 1966.

Willard, Frances E. and Mary A. Livermore, *American Woman,* Vol. I, New York: Mast Crowell & Kirkpatrick, 1897.

_____, *A Woman of the Century,* Chicago: Charles Wells Moulton, 1893.

Woman's Tribune, Beatrice, Nebraska.

Manuscript Collections

Women's Studies Manuscript Collections from the Schlesinger Library, Bethesda, Maryland: University Publications of America

Matilda Joslyn Gage Papers

Olympia Brown Collection

Anna Howard Shaw Papers

Records of the National American Woman Suffrage Association, Manuscript Division, Library of Congress

Holland, Patricia G. and Ann D. Gordon, eds. Papers of Elizabeth Cady Stanton and Susan B. Anthony

Papers of the New York State Woman Suffrage Association, Rare Books and Manuscript Division, Columbia University Library

About the Author

Mary E. Corey is an associate professor of American history and social studies education emerita at The College at Brockport, State University of New York. Her work combines scholarly interests in women's history and civil rights history.

Dr. Corey is also a faculty consultant for the Advanced Placement Exam in United States History through the College Board and has served on the Board of Trustees of the Brockport Community Museum. In addition, her work includes professional development workshops for secondary Advanced Placement teachers, "Using Artifacts in the Social Studies Classroom" at The Summer AP Institute at St. John Fisher College. She has conducted walking tours of historic Seneca Falls, N.Y., along with her video developed for these tours, "Weaving Women into the Curriculum." She has been active in the Teaching American History Program and with the National Center for Migrant Education. She has presented her research widely at the national and state levels including the Organization of American Historian's Annual Conferences, Researching New York Annual Conferences, and the Annual Conferences of the Association for the Study of African American Life and History.

Her most recent co-authored publications are the Faculty and Student editions of *Before Jackie: The Negro Leagues, Civil Rights, and the American Dream* and, individually, the high-school level textbooks, United States History, Parts I and II, for the National Center for Migrant Education. She lives in Western New York with her faithful companion, Bootsie Kitty Cat.